LOST CAUSES

LOST CAUSES

The Romantic Attraction of Defeated

Yet Unvanquished Men and Movements

GEORGE & KAREN GRANT

Cumberland House

NASHVILLE, TENNESSEE

Copyright © 1999 by George Grant and Karen Grant

Published by Cumberland House Publishing, Inc., 431 Harding Industrial Drive, Nashville, Tennessee 37211.

Jacket design by Tonya Presley
Text design by Bruce Gore, Gore Studios, Inc.

Library of Congress Cataloging-in-Publication Data

Grant, George, 1954–
    Lost causes : the romantic attraction of defeated yet unvanquished men and movements / George & Karen Grant.
        p.   cm.
    ISBN 1-58182-016-X (pbk. : alk. paper)
    1. Hope Quotations, maxims, etc.   2. History Quotations, maxims, etc.   3. Adversity Quotations, maxims, etc.   4. Defeat (Psychology) Quotations, maxims, etc.   I. Grant, Karen B., 1955–   II. Title.
PN6084.H62G73   1999
152.4—dc21   99-27143
                                                                            CIP

Printed in the United States of America
1 2 3 4 5 6 7 8 — 01 00 99 98 97

To the
Empty Hands Men
And Their Unvanquished Cause

CONTENTS

ACKNOWLEDGMENTS

*Everyone should consider himself as entrusted not only with his own
conduct, but with that of others; and as accountable, not only for the duties
he neglects or the crimes which he commits, but for the negligence and
irregularity which he may encourage or inculcate.*
SAMUEL JOHNSON (1709–1784)

Umberto Eco, the noted Italian semioticist and novelist, has written that "There is nothing more wonderful than a list, that instrument
of wondrous hypotyposis." Even a cursory glance at our writing reveals
that we are adherents of that time-honored medieval convention. Thus,
throughout our previous works you'll find lists of historical figures, lists
of literary texts, lists of practical applications, lists of authors and their
ideas, lists of movements and trends, and even lists of lists. Though this
is not necessarily a popular form of communication in these abbreviat-
ed, get-to-the-point, cut-to-the-chase modern times, it is nevertheless a
critical aspect of our own approach to life. Naturally then, this book
begins with a list: an enumeration of a whole host of dear friends, students, mentors, co-laborers, and family members who have loved us
well and supported us long.

Gene and Susan Hunt, Stephen and Tricia Mansfield, Tom and Jody Clark, Jim and Gwen Smith, Pete and Angela Volpitta, Hugh and Lisa Harris, Tom and Lucie Moucka, Terry and Gayle Cost, Mike and Dianne Tant, Robert and Kim Fulcher, Greg and Sophia Wilbur, and Anthony and Sharon Gordon have encouraged us in many a quixotic quest. And our students at Bannockburn College, Gileskirk School, and Franklin Classical School stood by us in many a lost cause.

Bill Lane, able theologian, loving mentor, brilliant conversationalist, and beloved friend, exhorted us to never lose sight of those eccentric passions for the lost causes of the past and the present. Indeed, it was Bill who told us that this book "has to be written. It is simply not an option."

The good folks at Cumberland House, and particularly our dear friends Ron and Julia Pitkin, embraced our vision for books that were distinctly practical, down-to-earth, fun, historically informed, nondidactic, and yet fully within the parameters of a Christian world-view. Perhaps that approach will be considered a lost cause in this odd moment of parenthesis in our culture—but it is one that must ultimately be vindicated.

To all these, we offer our sincerest thanks.

The soundtrack for this project—in other words, the music we were listening to as we wrote—was provided by the appropriately disparate music of Richard Searles, Orison, William Coulter, the Baltimore Consort, Anuna, and Mike Card. Likewise, the midnight musings—in other words, the books we were reading as we wrote—were provided by the equally diverse prose of James Blaylock, Tim Powers, Jan Karon, G. K. Chesterton, and Abraham Kuyper. Their influence, we hope, is obvious in both content and form.

As always though, it was our beloved children, Joel, Joanna, and Jesse, who most enabled us to write this very personal exploration of the perpetually defeated yet unvanquished. With nary a complaint, they sacrificed many a weekend as we struggled to squeeze some writing into an already too hectic schedule: We thank God upon every remembrance of you, always in every prayer of ours for you all making request with joy, for our fellowship in the Gospel from the first day until now; being confident of this very thing, that He which hath begun a good work in you will perform it until the day of Jesus Christ (Philippians 1:3–6).

In the end, that is perhaps the only justification that matters for any work, on any subject, in any discipline—regardless of whether it might be focused upon some hopelessly lost cause or just a list of a few of our favorite things.

ADVENT 1998
King's Meadow Farm

INTRODUCTION

"There is a friend that sticketh closer than a brother."
KING SOLOMON

H istory is replete with examples of great lost causes, ill-fated designs, subjugated aspirations that somehow continued to capture the imaginations, stir the passions, and tug at the sympathies of men and nations long after they had supposedly been vanquished. They seem to be those perpetually defeated things that nevertheless managed to survive their conquerors—instilling in their adherents eternal hope, blazing idealism, and irrepressible romanticism.

Alas, more recently, conscientious attachment to such honorable lost causes appears to have itself become yet another lost cause. Our blind faith in the tenants of modern pragmatism has made us rather intolerant of such things—to uphold their principles seems to be, at best, quixotic, at worst, foolhardy.

These days, everyone loves a winner. The sweet smell of success draws nearly all of us like moths to a candle flame. Popularity, celebrity, prominence, and fame are not only the hallmarks of our age, they are just about the only credentials we require for adulation or leadership.

As a result, we are generally not too terribly fond of the peculiar, the obscure, the romantic, the idealistic, or the unpopular. At best we reserve pity for dreamers, visionaries, and losers. In fact, we view with suspicion anyone who somehow fails to garner kudos from the world at large. If they have fallen prey to vilification, defamation, or humiliation we simply assume that they must somehow be at fault.

There was a time when martyrdom was among our civilization's highest callings and greatest honors. Early on, our progenitors embraced the truth that all those who desire to live forthrightly, steadfastly, and uncompromisingly would undoubtedly be forced to suffer the slings and arrows of discontent. The heroes of the past have always been those who actually sacrificed their lives, fortunes, and reputations for the sake of the truth.

But no longer. There is almost a kind of shame that we attach to those who suffer persecution or isolation in our culture. If their cause does not meet with quick success, we are only too hasty to abandon them. Maybe they didn't try hard enough. Maybe they just made a couple of dumb mistakes. Maybe they had faulty a philosophy or an errant theology. Maybe they just failed to marshal effective public relations techniques. But however they got into the mess they're in, we are all but certain that they are not the kind of models we ought to follow.

This is a particularly dangerous perspective given the fact that it was the commitment of stalwart men and women of hope to altogether hopeless causes that ultimately laid the foundations of freedom that we all enjoy today. Their struggles, sufferings, and failures have made possible our achievements, successes, and victories. Indeed, as E.M. Bounds, the great nineteenth century author who penned several classic books of inspiration, asserted, it is "all too often the case" that when we prosper "we lose sight of the very virtues from whence prosperity has sprung—virtues birthed in suffering, isolation, shame, and defeat."

Bounds found solace in the fact that our most important attachments in life need not depend on the confirmation of worldly notions of success and thus need not adjust to the ever-shifting tides of situation or circumstance. He knew that the blood, toil, tears, and sweat of the faithful are the seeds of real success and that our diligent, unflagging efforts on behalf of the despised and rejected, the defeated and denounced are often our most potent caveats to the worldly-wise.

The fact is, lasting victory in any arena of life cannot be won in a day, however fervently men may act. It takes time—perhaps generations. It has always been that way. It always will be.

Ultimately, this is why does an aura of romance has always found a way to attach itself to obviously defeated men and movements. It is why the idea somehow stubbornly persists—even in this relentlessly modern age—that failure is often a better and more encouraging example for us than success.

Some things are just worth fighting for. Even when the hope of victory is at best remote, some movements are worth staking our lives, our fortunes, and sacred honor on. Rooted in principle, driven by virtue, and sustained by deep and unswerving commitment, such romantic idealism, however impractical, seems to cast a stubborn spell over those who follow in later ages. And well it ought.

This book attempts to recover a sense of the continuing impact that lost causes might have on us today. It is an exploration of some noble men and movements that were defeated for a time, but whose principles and precepts have endured. It is an examination of those perpetually defeated things that have found a way—against all odds—to survive their conquerors.

Each chapter profiles a particular enduring virtue and some great lost cause that, to our minds at least, best exemplifies it. The poetry, epigrams, quotations, and excerpts are not merely anthologized illustrations. They are instead definitive—of both the virtue and the cause.

Admittedly this kind of book bears the inevitable stamp of subjective experience. In fact, it is the fourth in a series of books we've undertaken to exposit our very personal passions in life. *Letters Home* deals with the sage counsel of bygone days, *Best Friends* deals with the ways friendship shapes our lives, and *Just Visiting* deals with the way travel has enlightened lives and viewpoints throughout history. Yet to come are volumes on gardening, books, sports, food, and holiday celebrations. By its very nature, this book—like all the others in the series—is more a testimony than a documentary. These are our heroes. These are our causes. Our purpose in writing then, is to both express and profess.

According to the eighteenth century revolutionary pamphleteer, Thomas Paine, "That which we obtain too easily, we esteem too lightly. It is dearness only which gives everything its value—including successes which inevitably must venture through the sundry environs of defeats first. Heaven only knows how to put a proper price on its goods." This book is offered in the hope that we might esteem more highly those movements which have ventured through the environs of defeat. We believe that such a perspective is vital for these difficult days in which we live—days for which a few good lost causes might be a welcome relief from the smothering uniformity of too easily obtained successes.

Tradition

*W*e are enamoured of progress. We are at a time when things
shiny and new are prized far above things old and timeworn.
For most of us, tradition is little more than a quirky and nostalgic
sentimentalism. It is hardly more than the droning, monotonous
succession of obsolete notions, anachronous ideals, and antiquarian
habits—sound and fury, signifying nothing. Henry Ford called an
awareness of history and an appreciation for the past mere "bunk."
Augustine Birrell called it "a dust heap." Guy de Maupassant
dubbed it "that excitable and lying old lady." But many of the
wisest of men and women through the ages have recognized that
tradition is a foundation upon which all true advancement must be
built—that it is in fact the prerequisite to all genuine progress.

The greatest advances in human civilization have come when we recovered what we had lost: when we learned the lessons of history.

Winston Churchill (1874–1965)

A nation which does not remember what it was yesterday, does not know what it is today, nor what it is trying to do. We are trying to do a futile thing if we do not know where we came from or what we have been about. Ours is a rich legacy. Rich but lost.

Abraham Kuyper, 1837-1920

Those who have no concern for their ancestors will, by simple application of the same rule, have none for their descendants.

Richard Weaver (1910–1963)

A contempt of the monuments and the wisdom of the past, may be justly reckoned one of the reigning follies of these days, to which pride and idleness have equally contributed.

Samuel Johnson (1709–1784)

To comprehend the history of a thing is to unlock the mysteries of its present, and more, to disclose the profundities of its future.

ဧ| Hilaire Belloc (1870–1953) |ə

All our debate is voiceless here,
As all our rage, the rage of stone;
If hope is hopeless, then fearless fear,
And history is thus undone.

ဧ| Robert Penn Warren (1905–1989) |ə

In literature as in love, courage is half the battle. Likewise, in virtue as in fashion, tradition is the surest guide to the future.

ဧ| Sir Walter Scott (1771–1832) |ə

In history's mixture of good and evil, the thing we should note—the thing the historians will note with amazement—is the profundity and the rapidity of change.

ဧ| Hilaire Belloc (1870–1953) |ə

Clearly, in order to advance the cause of life and liberty in these dark and difficult days, we must recover what we have lost—we must learn the lessons of history. There is no need for us to attempt to reinvent the wheel. The battles for truth, justice, and mercy have been fought again and again and again. Successfully. We need not cast about for direction. We need not grope in the dark for strategies, programs, and agendas. We need not manufacture new ideas, new priorities, or new tactics. We already have a tested and proven formula for victory. We already have a winning legacy. We simply need to reclaim it. We simply need to recover what is rightfully ours.

Tristan Gylberd (1954–)

Intent on its ending, they are ignorant of its beginning; and therefore of its very being.

G. K. Chesterton (1874–1936)

Both the liberals and the conservatives have lost definition. Neither one can make us know what a tradition might.

Andrew Nelson Lytle (1902–1995)

Custom reconciles us to everything.

Edmund Burke (1729–1797)

There are those who believe that a new modernity demands a new morality. What they fail to consider is the harsh reality that there is no such thing as a new morality. There is only one morality. All else is immorality. There is only true Christian ethics over against which stands the whole of paganism. If we are to fulfill our great destiny as a people, then we must return to the old morality, the sole morality.

Theodore Roosevelt (1858–1919)

The great ancients' writings, beside ours,
Look like illuminated manuscripts
Before plain press type.

Philip James Bailey (1816–1902)

There is the moral of all human tales;
'Tis but the same rehearsal of the past,
First freedom, then glory—when that fails,
Wealth, vice, corruption—barbarism at last,
And history, with all her volumes vast,
Hath but one page.

Lord Byron (1788–1824)

You can never dictate the future by the past—you may, however, ameliorate its illest effects and heighten its greatest delights by its remembrance.

Edmund Burke (1729–1797)

As counsel of both times—of the ancient time what is best, and of the latter time what is fittest.

Francis Bacon (1561–1626)

The recollection of the past is only useful by way of provision for the future.

Samuel Johnson (1709–1784)

Those who are in rebellion against memory are the ones who wish to live without knowledge.

Richard Weaver (1910—1963)

People will not look forward to posterity who will not look backward to their ancestors.

Edmund Burke (1729–1797)

Tradition wears a snowy beard,
Romance is always young.

John Greenleaf Whittier (1807–1892)

Time after time mankind is driven against the rocks of the horrid reality of a fallen creation. And time after time mankind must learn the hard lessons of history—the lessons that for some dangerous and awful reason we can't seem to keep in our collective memory.

Hilaire Belloc (1870–1953)

Weak things must boast of being new, like so many new German philosophies. But strong things can boast of being old. Strong things can boast of being moribund.

G. K. Chesterton (1874–1936)

It is always surprising to the uninitiated, the power that lies in essential and primordial things—discredited though they may be by the concourse of modernity.

Richard Weaver (1910–1963)

All heaven and earth resound with that subtle and delicately balanced truth that the old paths are the best paths after all.

J. C. Ryle (1816–1900)

Every tradition grows ever more venerable—the more remote its origin, the more confused that origin is. The reverence due to it increases from generation to generation. The tradition finally becomes holy and inspires awe. Is this ill or fine? If the accumulated wisdom and the tested habits of the ages accounts for naught, then surely it is ill. But if such things afford security and sanity, then it is an augur of great good. Sense and sensibility should sway us toward the confident latter and not the impetuous former.

James Gleason Archer (1844–1909)

A ruin should always be protected but never repaired—thus may we witness full the lingering legacies of the past.

Sir Walter Scott (1771–1832)

Just as a loss of memory in an individual is a psychiatric defect calling for medical treatment, so too any community which has no social memory is suffering from an illness.

John H. Y. Briggs (1922–)

History must be our deliverer not only from the undue influence of other times, but from the undue influence of our own, from the tyranny of the environment and the pressures of the air we breathe.

Lord Acton (1834–1902)

The prevailing spirit of the present age seems to be the spirit of skepticism and captiousness, of suspicion and distrust in private judgment; a dislike of all established forms, merely because they are established, and of old paths, because they are old.

Samuel Johnson (1709–1784)

Modernism is in essence a provincialism, since it declines to look beyond the horizon of the moment.

Richard Weaver (1910–1963)

The antiquary of tradition is the preserver of all that is right and good and true. It is the wisest and most progressive of all the human impulses—for it guarantees continuity for the uncertain days of the future. Let every man and woman warmly embrace the lessons of the past.

Calvin Coolidge (1872–1933)

Sir Walter Scott and the Importance of the Past

His life was a monument to the vitality of heritage. His writing captured the essence of the heroism, romanticism, and dynamism of the past. His character was a testimony to the vibrant virtues of days gone by. His habits recalled the rites and rituals of a hoary yore. Even his home was a saga in stone, a ballad of yesteryear in pitch and gable and crenellation, and a reliquary of legend, fable, and custom. Everything about Sir Walter Scott bespoke tradition.

He was born in 1771 to a respectable middle class Edinburgh family, but much of his childhood was spent at his grandfather's farm in the beautiful Border country. It was there that he was first acquainted with the rituals, songs, ballads, folklore, and legends of Scotland that captivated him for the rest of his life.

He demonstrated early genius and followed in his father's footsteps, becoming a barrister after completing his university training at the extraordinary age of seventeen. But practice of the law was not able to fully occupy his precocious mind, and so he began the work of translating his favorite historical novels and poems of Bürger and Goethe from the original German. This literary work proved to be exhilarating to him, satisfying both his artistic bent and his great love for the legend and lore of the past.

Before long he was composing original verse and collecting the great ballads of his beloved Border lands. He composed a great narrative poem, *The Lay of the Last Minstrel*, which proved to be a tremendous commercial and critical success—and that convinced him that literature should be the main business of his life.

Happily married and with a growing family to support, he determined to pursue the literary life away from the constant and pressing demands of the city. He bought a large farm along the Tweed valley in the Border countryside. He called it Abbotsford, and for the rest of his life he made the house, the grounds, the furnishings, and the library a living demonstration of his highest ideals and loftiest ambitions. Over the years he transformed the humble farmhouse into a magnificent castle estate chock-a-block with remnants, relics, and reminders of the rich history of the region. There was an armory with the weapons of Rob Roy. There was a chapel with the devotional books of Mary Queen of Scots, there was a study with the pens of Robert Burns, there was a library with furniture carved from wood recovered from the Spanish Armada, and there was a garden with the roses of Eleanor of Aquitaine.

It was there in his museum-like environs that he created a series of historical novels that made Scott the most popular author in the world. Beginning with *Waverly* in 1814 and continuing through an astonishing thirty-two volumes over the next eighteen years—and including such classics as *Ivanhoe*, *Rob Roy*, *Tales of a Grandfather*, *Old Mortality*, *The Antiquarian*, and *Red Gauntlet*—Scott reinvented an entire genre of literature.

He added immeasurably to the Scottish sense of identity. Indeed, he almost single-handedly revived interest in kilts, tartans, Gaelic, bagpipes, Highland dancing, haggis, Celtic music, and all the other distinctive elements of Scottish culture. Tales of the Covenanters, Wallace and Bruce, the Jacobites, Bonnie Prince Charlie, and Rob Roy were all brought into the light of day by his intrepid commitment to regaling the past.

All of his books were stamped with his overarching conviction about the importance of tradition. He believed with utmost fervency that the map of

God's activity in the world was not a blank ocean between the apostolic shores and the modern day. Thus it was imperative that men and nations remember—and search for their roots in—the luminaries, the risk takers, and great movements through the centuries. To neglect them, he believed, was not only to risk repeating past errors, it was to fall victim to a narrowing amnesia that necessarily leaves whole civilizations floundering.

On the cusp of the magnificent flowering of industrial advance, it seemed to Scott that men were sadly afflicted with a kind of malignant contemporaneity. He was alarmed that their morbid preoccupation with self—and thus their ambivalence and ignorance of the past—had trapped them in a recalcitrant present.

The nineteenth century produced steamships, railroads, streetcars, bicycles, rollerskates, the air brake, the torpedo, telephones, telegraphs, transatlantic cables, harvesting machines, threshers, cotton gins, cooking ranges, sewing machines, phonographs, typewriters, electric lights, illuminating gas, photographs, x-rays, motion pictures, and cottonseed oil. According to journalist Edward Byrn, the comparison of the start of the century with the end of the century was "like the juxtaposition of a distant star with the noonday sun." And popular historian M. J. de Forest Shelton exclaimed in all truthfulness, that there was "more difference between Napoleon's day and ours than between Napoleon's and Julius Caesar's. One century against eighteen." Agreeing, the English intellectual Frederic Harrison, said, "Take it all in all, the merely material, physical, mechanical change in human life in the hundred years, from the days of Watt and Arkwright to our own, is greater than occurred in the thousand years that preceded, perhaps even the two thousand or twenty thousand years."

In the midst of such whirling change, Scott was committed to the efficacy of tradition to offer stability, continuity, and guidance. He knew only too well that connections to the past were the only sure leads to the future. He was adamant about the notion that history was not just the concern of historians and social scientists. It was not the lonely domain of political prognosticators and ivory tower academics. It was the very stuff of life. And, in fact, he believed it was the very stuff of faith. He was always taken by the fact that the Bible put a heavy emphasis on historical awareness—not at all surprising considering the fact that the vast proportion of its own contents record the dealings of God with men and nations throughout the ages.

Again and again he recalled that stress in the Scriptures, God calls upon His people to remember: He calls on them to remember the bondage, oppression, and deliverance of Egypt; He calls on them to remember the splendor, strength, and devotion of the Davidic Kingdom; He calls on them to remember the valor, forthrightness, and holiness of the prophets; He calls on them to remember the glories of creation, the devastation of the flood, the judgment of the great apostasies, the miraculous events of the exodus, the anguish of the desert wanderings, the grief of the Babylonian exile, the responsibility of the restoration, the sanctity of the Lord's Day, the graciousness of the commandments, and the ultimate victory of the cross; He calls on them to remember the lives and witness of all those who have gone before in faith—forefathers, fathers, patriarchs, prophets, apostles, preachers, evangelists, martyrs, confessors, ascetics, and every righteous spirit made pure in Christ. Indeed, he believed that remembrance and forgetfulness were the measuring rods of faithfulness throughout the entire canon of Scripture—that is why the Bible makes it plain that there are only two kinds of people in the world: effectual doers and forgetful hearers.

As a result, all of Scott's work essentially argued that stable societies must be eternally vigilant in the task of handing on their great legacy—to remember and then to inculcate that remembrance in the hearts and minds of their children. He made the venerable aphorism, "He who forgets his own history is condemned to repeat it," his personal and professional credo. He was certain that any people who did not know their own history would simply have to endure all the same mistakes, sacrifices, and absurdities all over again.

Sadly, such lessons are very nearly lost on us in this odd to-whom-it-may-concern, instant-everything day of microwavable meals, prefab buildings, bottom-rung bureaucracy, fit-for-the-market education, knee-jerk public misinformation, and predigested formula entertainment. Thus temporary expediencies supersede permanent exigencies. Thus, at a time when tradition gets a rather short shrift, when traditionalism is all but a lost cause, it would stand us in good stead to once again give heed to the life and legacy of Sir Walter Scott.

I have heard higher sentiments from the lips of the poor uneducated men and women, when exerting the spirit of severe yet gentle heroism under difficulties and afflictions, or speaking their simple thoughts as to circumstances in the lot of friends and neighbors, than I ever met with out of the pages of the Bible. My firm conviction is that they have the advantage of never being separated from tradition by the fopperies of fashion.

Sir Walter Scott (1771–1832)

Work

Most of us do not much care for work. We complain about it. We chaff against it. We will do just about anything to get out of it. Nevertheless, we probably would reluctantly admit that nearly everything in life worth anything at all demands of us a certain measure of labor and intensity. And though this might appear at first glance to be a plight of woe and hardship—perhaps a deleterious effect of the Fall—it is in fact a part of the glory of the human experience. The good news is that work is good. The good news is that the lost cause of diligent labor, strenuous industry, and purposeful calling may be reclaimed, restored, and reinstituted—as the examples of so many wise men and women who have gone before so ably and aptly demonstrate.

I wish to preach not the doctrine of ignoble ease but the doctrine of the strenuous life; the life of toil and effort; of labor and strife; to preach that highest form of success which comes not to the man who desires mere easy peace but to the man who does not shrink from danger, hardship, or from the bitter toil, and who out of these wins the splendid ultimate triumph.

Theodore Roosevelt (1858–1919)

I long to accomplish a great and noble task, but it is my chief duty to accomplish humble tasks as though they were great and noble. The world is moved along not by the mighty shoves of its heroes, but by the aggregate of the tiny pushes of each honest worker.

Helen Keller (1880–1968)

When idle, be not solitary; when solitary, be not idle.

Samuel Johnson (1709–1784)

The process has been long, to some extent tedious, but profitable, because insomuch as it has taken time and care and intelligence, by that much does it have a meaning.

Andrew Nelson Lytle (1902–1995)

Never get into a rut. You cannot afford to do a thing poorly. You are more injured in shirking your work or half-doing a job than the person for whom you are working.

Booker T. Washington (1856–1915)

Exertion, self-denial, endurance, these make the hero, but to the spoiled child they connote the evil of nature and the malice of man.

Richard Weaver (1910–1963)

If you have a job without aggravations, you don't have a job.

Malcolm Forbes (1919–1990)

The world desires to know what a man can do, not what he knows.

Booker T. Washington (1856–1915)

The idle man does not know what it is to enjoy rest.

Albert Einstein (1879–1955)

My son, ill-gotten gains do not profit, but righteousness delivers from death. The Lord will not allow the righteous to hunger, but He will thrust aside the craving of the wicked. Poor is he who works with a negligent hand, but the hand of the diligent makes rich. The soul of the sluggard craves and gets nothing, but the soul of the diligent is made fat. Wealth obtained by fraud dwindles, but the one who gathers by labor increases it. A man can do nothing better than find satisfaction in his work.

King Solomon (c. 1000 B.C.)

Our Savior, Christ Jesus, was a carpenter and got His living with great labor. Therefore, let no man disdain to follow Him in a common calling and occupation.

Hugh Latimer (1485–1555)

The world does not consider labor a blessing, therefore, it flees and hates it but the pious who fear the Lord, labor with a ready and cheerful heart; for they know God's command and will, they acknowledge His calling.

Martin Luther (1483–1546)

Leaders are those who make the most of every moment, of every opportunity, and of every available resource.

Theodore Roosevelt (1858–1919)

If you get into the habit of putting in hard and conscientious work, doing a little duty well, no matter how insignificant; if you get into the habit of doing well whatever falls to your hands, whether in the light or in the dark—you will find that you are going to lay a foundation for success.
Booker T. Washington (1856–1915)

A Christian should follow his occupation with contentment. Is your business here clogged with any difficulties and inconveniences? Contentment under those difficulties is no little part of your homage to that King who hath placed you where you are by His call.
Cotton Mather (1663–1728)

We know that all men were created to busy themselves with labor for the common good.
John Calvin (1509–1564)

As pride sometimes is hid under humility, idleness is often covered by turbulence and hurry.
Samuel Johnson (1709–1784)

If we look externally there is a difference betwixt the washing of dishes and preaching of the Word of God; but as touching to please God, in relation to His call, none at all.

William Tyndale (1494–1536)

Genius is seldom recognized for what it is: a great capacity for hard work.

Henry Ford (1863–1947)

Work is much more fun than fun.

Noel Coward (1899–1973)

A man can do nothing better than to find satisfaction in his work.

King Solomon (c. 1000 B.C.)

All stations are so oriented that they serve others.

Martin Luther (1483–1546)

We may not like to admit it, but work is the heart and soul, the corner-stone, of man's created purpose. It is the basis of all ministry and it is the foundation upon which true compassion is built. God's first word to man through Moses was definitive: Be fruitful and increase in number; fill the earth and subdue it. Rule over the fish of the sea and the birds of the air. Have dominion over every living creature that moves on the ground. In other words: work. Far from being a bitter consequence of the Fall, work is a vital aspect of God's overall purpose for man in space and time. For that reason, He has typically used workmen, ordinary laborers, in the enactment of that purpose. He has used shepherds like Jacob and David. He has used farmers like Amos and Gideon. He has used merchants like Abraham and Lydia. He has used craftsmen like Aquilla and Paul. He has used artists like Solomon and Bezalel. And the men He chose to revolutionize the Roman Empire in the first century were a motley band of fishermen and tax collectors.

Tristan Gylberd (1954–)

He has lived with little observation either on himself or others, who does not know that to be idle is to be vicious.

Samuel Johnson (1709–1784)

Man was made for work. The Fall unmade him. Now, in Christ made anew, man can once again work. But he must be ever mindful of the salvific connection: the call to work must not, cannot, go out unaccompanied by the call to salvation.

Langdon Lowe (1843–1919)

Work is not just to benefit ourselves. By work, we are to uphold our responsibility to provide for our family, build the work of Christ's Kingdom, and share with those in need. Work is mercy.

Tristan Gylberd (1954–)

BOOKER T. WASHINGTON AND THE RECONCILIATION OF THE LAND

The centerpiece of the Tuskegee University campus in southern Alabama is the Booker T. Washington monument. Upon a grand classical pedestal stands a remarkable bronze statue sculpted by Charles Keck in 1922. Washington himself is portrayed—stately, dignified, and venerable—standing with his eyes set upon the horizon while one hand is extended toward the future. With the other hand he is resolutely pulling back a thick veil—presumably the smothering cloak of Strabo—from the brow of a young man seated at his side. The man is obviously poor—he is only half-clothed, in stark contrast to the dapper presence of Washington—and is sitting upon the symbols of his labor, an anvil and a plow. But he too is gazing off into the distance while he grasps a massive academic textbook upon his knee. The inscription beneath this arresting image asserts, "He lifted the veil of ignorance from his people and pointed the way to progress through education and industry."

The monument is a perfect tribute to the man. While his life—the long and difficult journey up from the obscurity of slavery to the heights of national influence and renown—is a remarkable testimony of individual achievement and personal sacrifice, the greatest legacy of Booker T. Washington was not what he accomplished himself, but what he helped thousands of others to accomplish—both black and white.

He was born on April 5, 1856, on a small tobacco plantation in the back country of Franklin County, Virginia. His nine years in slavery were spent in abject poverty—though it was hardly worse than the hardscrabble existence of his poor masters. And while the terribly uncivil war that wracked the region in those early years brought even more hardship and privation, there was a sense of anticipation and excitement among the slaves. They even spoke openly about the possibilities of the freedom that might come if the Yankee armies succeeded in their invasion and subjugation of the South. And though their prayers were answered, even after the war the poverty of most slaves remained unabated. Young Washington's first memories then were of the difficult and dire straits his family was forced to endure.

He had always had a deep and abiding hunger to learn despite the fact that he was not afforded the opportunity to go to school until he was practically in his teens. When he was sixteen, he gained admittance to the Hampton Institute—one of the first schools established for former slaves. Although he worked full-time as a janitor to pay his tuition, he graduated with honors in a mere three years. Upon graduation, he returned to his family and taught in the local grammar school.

Before long, his mentor at Hampton beckoned him to return to that institution where he became an instructor and assistant to the president. Shortly afterward the state of Alabama contacted the school about the possibility of establishing a similar college. Washington was recommended for the job. Thus, on July 4, 1881, at the age of twenty-five, Washington founded Tuskegee.

The obstacles facing him were enormous. There was no money, no faculty, no campus, no land, and no student body. Indeed, there was nothing except the resolution of the state to launch the school and the determination of Booker T. Washington to raise up a whole new generation of leaders from the rubble of the South and the legacy of slavery. Nevertheless, before his death in 1915, Tuskegee had grown to encompass a two-thou

sand acre campus of 107 buildings with more than fifteen-hundred students
and nearly two-hundred faculty members. More importantly though,
Washington had instilled his philosophy of hard work, competence, and
community-mindedness in thousands of students all across the country who
were at last making a substantive difference in the welfare of African-
American families, churches, neighborhoods, and businesses.

Washington made certain that the curriculum of the school not only
emphasized the traditional academic disciplines, but also the virtues of
industry, cleanliness, and personal morality. He believed that ultimately, if
young black students could learn these lessons, they could make themselves
indispensable to their communities—thus accomplishing more to end dis-
crimination, segregation, and prejudice than any political program of civil
rights ever might.

Besides the grammar, logic, and rhetoric of a standard classical education which they received there, the students at Tuskegee built virtually all
of the buildings—they even made and fired the bricks and cut and hewed
the timbers used to construct them. They manufactured the pillows and
mattresses used in the dormitory. They tilled the soil and tended the crops
in the campus gardens. They cooked the food served in the cafeteria.
Indeed, all students were expected to acquire a practical knowledge of at
least one trade together with the spirit of industry, thrift, and economy necessary to make an honest living after they graduated.

As a result of his efforts, Washington became a celebrity, much in
demand as a speaker and lecturer around the country and as a consultant
and confidant to powerful politicians and community leaders. Though he
was criticized by some because he refused to use his influence for direct

political agitation, he had obviously begun the long process toward the reconciliation of long sundered communities and races.

He argued in his famous speech at the Cotton States' Exposition in Atlanta in 1895:

"Ignorant and inexperienced, it is not strange that in the first years of our new life we began at the top instead of at the bottom; that a seat in Congress or the state legislature was more sought than real estate or industrial skill; that the political convention or stump speaking had more attractions than starting a dairy farm or truck garden. A ship lost at sea for many days suddenly sighted a friendly vessel. From the mast of the unfortunate vessel was seen a signal: *Water, water; we die of thirst!* The answer from the friendly vessel at once came back: *Cast down your bucket where you are.* And a third and fourth signal for water was answered, *Cast down your bucket where you are.* The captain of the distressed vessel, at last heeding the injunction, cast down his bucket, and it came up full of fresh, sparkling water from the mouth of the Amazon River. To those of my race who depend on bettering their condition in a foreign land or who underestimate the importance of cultivating friendly relations with the Southern white man, who is their next-door neighbor, I would say: *Cast down your bucket where you are*—cast it down in making friends in every manly way of the people of all races by whom we are surrounded. Cast it down in agriculture, mechanics, in commerce, in domestic service, and in the professions. And in this connection it is well to bear in mind that whatever other sins the South may be called to bear, when it comes to business, pure and simple, it is in the South that the Negro is given a man's chance in the commercial world, and in nothing is this exposition more eloquent than in emphasizing this chance. Our greatest danger is that in the great leap from slavery to freedom we may overlook the fact that the masses of us are to live by the productions of our hands, and fail to keep in mind that we shall prosper in proportion as we learn to dignify and glorify common labor and put brains and skill into the common occupations of life; shall prosper in proportion as we learn to draw the line between the superficial and the substantial, the ornamental gew-gaws of life and the useful. No race can prosper till it learns that there is as much dignity in tilling a field as in writing a poem. It is at the bottom of life we must begin, and not at the top. Nor should we permit our grievances to overshadow our opportunities. To those of the white race who look to the incoming of those of foreign birth and strange tongue and habits for the prosperity of the South, were I permitted I would repeat what I say to my own race, "Cast down your bucket where you are." Cast it down among the eight millions of Negroes whose habits you know, whose fidelity and love you have tested in days when to have proved treacherous meant the ruin of your firesides. Cast down your bucket among these people who have, without strikes and labor wars, tilled your fields, cleared your forests, built your railroads and cities, and brought forth treasures from the bowels of the earth, and helped make possible this magnificent representation of the progress of the South. Casting down your bucket among my people, helping and encouraging them as you are doing on these grounds, and to education of head, hand, and heart, you will find that they will buy your surplus land, make blossom the waste places in your fields, and run your factories. While doing this, you can be sure in the future, as in the past, that you and your families will be surrounded by the most patient, faithful, law-abiding, and unresentful people that the world has seen. As we have proved our loyalty to you in the past, in nursing your children, watching by the sick-bed of your mothers and fathers, and often following them with tear-dimmed eyes to their graves, so in the future, in our humble way, we shall stand by you with a devotion that no foreigner can approach, ready to lay down our lives, if need be, in defense of yours, interlacing our industrial, commercial, civil, and religious life with yours in a way that shall make the interests of both races one. In all things that are purely social we can be as separate as the fingers, yet one as the hand in all things essential to mutual progress. There is no defense or security for any of us except in the highest intelligence and development of all. If anywhere there are efforts tending to curtail the fullest growth of the Negro, let these efforts be turned into stimulating, encouraging, and making him the most useful and intelligent citizen. Effort or means so invested will pay a thousand percent interest. These efforts will be twice blessed—blessing him that gives and him that takes. There is no escape through law of man or God from the inevitable: The laws of changeless justice bind oppressor with oppressed. And close as sin and suffering joined, we march to fate abreast."

Alas, following his death, his critics seemed to gain the upper hand in most civil rights organizations and institutions. Though he was a tremendous influence on Dr. Martin Luther King Jr., most other black leaders of the twentieth century preferred a more radical and direct approach—a forthrightly ideological and political approach—to social and cultural change. But the continued exasperation of racial relations, the devastation of the African-American family, and the deterioration of black opportunity and mobility over the last forty years or so has brought renewed interest in Washington's vision of reconciliation through the long but fruitful work of community building, industry, and family integrity. The great lost cause of the Tuskegee way seems to be reemerging as the twentieth century comes to an end. Prominent black leaders like Thomas Sowell, Walter Williams, Clarence Thomas, J. C. Watt, and Alan Keyes have revived the example of Booker T. Washington in the hopes that his vision might finally and fully be implemented.

Reconciling the land is no easy feat. Not by any stretch of the imagination. But then, Washington never pretended that such a noble aspiration would be achieved easily or without great sacrifice. Success would come, he was certain, only after diligent labor, strenuous industry, and purposeful calling were applied in our lives, our families, and our communities. Such defeated yet unvanquished principles are hardly popular these days. But if they are revived, perhaps then the smothering cloak of Strabo may be lifted once and for all.

I have learned that success is to be measured not so much by the position that one has reached in life, as by the obstacles which he has overcome while trying to succeed.

Booker T. Washington (1856–1915)

Mercy

*T*hese days, it appears that the concept of service has all but replaced the old virtue of mercy. Good service, we are told, guarantees customer loyalty, management efficiency, and employee morale. Political candidates now offer themselves for public service rather than to merely run for office. Alas, service is thus defined rather broadly in a series of happy platitudes—as an expansive sense of public-spiritedness, good neighborliness, community-mindedness, or big-hearted cooperativeness. While admirable, such notions are a far cry from the venerable assumption of merciful selflessness that once gave vitality to our communities. Mercy isn't a tactic designed to boost profit margins, to protect market shares, to keep customers happy, or to garner votes. It isn't a style of leadership, a personality bent, or a habit of highly effective people. Wise men and women through the ages have understood only too well that it is a means of caring for our neighbors and offering them kindness in times of distress. The great lost cause of mercy is far more concerned about taking care of souls than about taking care of business.

Let your hand feel for the afflictions and distresses of everyone, and let your hand give in proportion to your purse; remembering always the estimation of the widow's mite, that it is not everyone that asketh that deserveth charity; all however are worthy of the inquiry, or the deserving may suffer. Thus is the mettle of true character.

George Washington (1732–1799)

Mercy offers whatever is necessary to heal the hurts of others.

Dolly Madison (1768–1849)

Train your tongue to offer solace, your heart to offer sympathy, and your hand to offer mercy.

Peter Lorimer (1812–1879)

Lay hold of something that will help you, and then use it to help somebody else.

Booker T. Washington (1856–1915)

Mercy has converted more souls than zeal, or eloquence, or learning or all of them together.

Søren Kierkegaard (1813–1855)

And I will gladly share with you your pain,
If it turn out I can no comfort bring;
For tis a friend's right, please let me explain,
To share in woeful as in joyful things.
Geoffrey Chaucer (1343–1400)

Merciful service gives itself rich; selfish isolation hoards itself poor.
Theodore Roosevelt (1858–1919)

Be merciful, just as your Father is merciful.
Jesus Christ (c. 1–33)

Do unto others as if you were others.
Leonardo da Vinci (1452–1519)

Mercy is two hearts tugging at one load.
Sarah Orne Jewett (1849–1909)

This is pure and undefiled religion in the sight of our God and Father, to visit the orphans and widows in their distress and to keep oneself unstained by the world.

James of Jerusalem (c. 4–46)

Love is like the wild rose-briar;
Friendship like the holly-tree.
The holly is dark when the rose-briar blooms,
But which will bloom most constantly?

The wild rose-briar is sweet in spring,
In summer blossoms scent the air,
Yet wait till winter comes again
And who will call the wild-briar fair?

Then scorn the silly rose-wreath now
And deck thee with the holly's sheen,
That when December blights thy brow
He still may leave thy garland green.

Emily Brontë (1818–1848)

For the grace of God has appeared, bringing salvation to all men, instructing us to deny ungodliness and worldly desires, and to live sensibly, righteously and godly in the present age, looking for the blessed hope and the appearing of the glory of our great God and Savior, Christ Jesus; who gave Himself for us, that He might redeem us from every lawless deed and purify for Himself a people for His own possession, zealous for good deeds.

Paul of Tarsus (c. 10–65)

How easy is it for one benevolent being to diffuse pleasure around him, and how truly is a kind heart a fountain of gladness, making everything in its vicinity to freshen into smiles.

Washington Irving (1783–1859)

Where there are no good works, there is no faith. If works and love do not blossom forth, it is not genuine faith, the Gospel has not yet gained a foothold, and Christ is not yet rightly known.

Martin Luther (1483–1546)

Good works, done in obedience to God's commandments, are the fruits and evidences of a true and lively faith: and by them believers manifest their thankfulness, strengthen their assurance, edify their brethren, adorn the profession of the Gospel, stop the mouths of the adversaries, and glorify God whose workmanship they are, created in Christ Jesus thereunto; that, having their fruit unto holiness, they may have in the end, eternal life.

George Gillespie (1613–1648)

Mercy is the golden chain by which society is bound together.

William Blake (1757–1827)

Sowing mercy is life's best investment.

Malcolm Forbes (1919–1990)

We in America can attain our great destiny only by service; not by rhetoric, and above all not by insincere rhetoric, and that dreadful mental double-dealing and verbal juggling which makes promises and repudiates them, and says one thing at one time, and the directly opposite thing at another time. Our service must be the service of deeds.

Theodore Roosevelt (1858–1919)

Always, sir, set a high value on spontaneous kindness. He whose inclination prompts him to cultivate your friendship of his own accord, will love you more than one whom you have been at pains to attach to.

ↄɬ *Samuel Johnson (1709–1784)* ɬo

Kindly affections,
And gentle ministrations,
Hallowed intimacies,
And generous sympathies:
Such are the appliances
Of trust;
Such are the devices
Of friendship.

ↄɬ *Tristan Gylberd (1954–)* ɬo

That religion which God requires, and will accept, does not consist in weak, dull, lifeless wishes, raising us but a little above a state of indifference. God in His Word, greatly insists upon it, that we be in good earnest, fervent in spirit, and our hearts vigorously engaged in mercies.

ↄɬ *Jonathan Edwards (1703–1758)* ɬo

God's intent in endowing any person with more substance than he needs is that he may have the pleasurable office, or rather the delightful privilege, of relieving want and woe. Alas, how many there are who consider that store which God has put into their hands on purpose for the poor and needy, to be only so much provision for their excessive luxury, a luxury which pampers them but yields them neither benefit nor pleasure. Others dream that wealth is given them that they may keep it under lock and key, cankering and corroding, breeding covetousness and care. Who dares roll a stone over the well's mouth when thirst is raging all around? Who dares keep the bread from the women and children who are ready to gnaw their own arms for hunger? Above all, who dares allow the sufferer to writhe in agony uncared for, and the sick to pine into their graves unnursed? This is no small sin: it is a crime to be answered for, to the Judge, when He shall come to judge the quick and the dead.

Charles H. Spurgeon (1834–1892)

The chief spiritual works in the world are sevenfold: to admonish sinners, to instruct the ignorant, to counsel the doubtful, to comfort the sorrowful, to suffer wrongs patiently, to forgive injuries, and to pray for all men at all times. Thus, we are to feed the hungry, give drink to the thirsty, to clothe the naked, to ransom the captives, to shelter the homeless, to visit the sick, and to rescue the perishing, for only in these corporal acts of service may this world of carnality be guarded from the full consequences of judgment.

Sava of Trnova (c. 675–728)

If I can stop one heart from breaking,
I shall not live in vain;
If I can ease one life the aching,
Or cool one pain,
Or help one fainting robin
Unto his nest again,
I shall not live in vain.

Emily Dickinson (1830–1886)

He has shown you, O man, what is good and what the Lord requires of you: but to do justice, and to love mercy, and to walk humbly with your God.

Micah of Moreseth (c. 700 B.C.)

Nothing costs so little, goes so far, and accomplishes so much as a single act of merciful service.

Auguste Renoir (1841–1919)

If you have a friend worth loving,
Love him. Yes, and let him know
That you love him, ere life's evening
Tinge his brow with sunset glow.
Why should good words ne'er be said
Of a friend—till he is dead?

If you hear a song that thrills you
Sung by any child of song,
Praise it. Do not let the singer
Wait deserved praises long.
Why should one who thrills your heart
Lack the joy you may impart?

If you hear a prayer that moves you
By its humble pleading tone,
Join it. Do not let the seeker
Bow before his God alone.
Why should not your brother share
The strength of "two or three" in prayer?

If you see hot tears falling
From a brother's weeping eyes,
Share them. And by kindly sharing

Own our kinship in the skies.
Why should anyone be glad
When a brother's heart is sad?

If a silvery laugh goes rippling
Through the sunshine on his face,
Share it. 'Tis the wise man's saying:
For both grief and joy a place.
There's health and goodness in the mirth
In which an honest laugh has birth.

If your work is made more easy
By a friendly, helping hand,
Say so. Speak out brave and truly
Ere the darkness veil the land.
Should a brother workman dear
Falter for a word of cheer?

Scatter thus your seeds of kindness
All enriching as you go:
Leave them. Trust the Harvest Giver;
He will make each seed to grow.
So until the happy end
Your life shall never lack a friend.

Alexander MacLeod (1786–1869)

The Modern world is full of the old Christian virtues gone mad. The virtues have gone mad because they have been isolated from each other and are wandering alone. Thus some scientists care for truth; but their truth is pitiless. And thus some humanitarians care only for pity; but their pity—I am sorry to say—is often untruthful.

G. K. Chesterton (1874–1936)

A lot of people mean well, but their meanness is greater than their wellness.

Robert Hunter (1823–1897)

There are two ways: the way of life and the way of death, and the difference between these two ways is great.

Didache (c. 100)

The quality of mercy is not strained,
It droppeth as the gentle rain from Heaven
Upon the place beneath; it is twice blessed;
It blesseth him that gives and him that takes:
'Tis the mightiest in the mightiest; it becomes
The throned monarch better than his crown;
His scepter shows the force of temporal power,
The attribute to awe and majesty,
Wherein doth sit the dread and fear of kings,
But mercy is above this sceptered sway,
It is enthronèd in the hearts of kings,
It is an attribute to God Himself,
And earthly power doth then show likest God's
When mercy seasons justice.

William Shakespeare (c. 1564–1616)

You shall love your neighbor more than your own life.

Barnabas of Antioch (c. 180)

This day,
In sadness borne,
We must confess:
The Spirit of the Age
Has crushed
The infant in the cradle.
And yet:
O glorious yet,
One day, in gladness shown,
We must profess:
The infant from the manger
Has crushed
The Spirit of the Age.

Tristan Gylberd (1954–)

Dympna of Gheel and the Love of the Unlovely

Caught between two worlds—the world of a frighteningly dark primordial barbarism and the world of a bright hopeful Christian civilization— Dympna Caelrhynn was born near the end of the eighth century, the eldest daughter of a heathen Celtic prince, Eadburh. When she was still just a child, her beloved Christian mother was claimed by a plague. Apparently stricken mad with grief, Eadburh conceived a perverted passion for his daughter. In order to escape his incestuous intentions, she fled abroad with her chaplain Gerebernus, first to the newly Christianized port city of Antwerp, and then to the small village of Gheel about twenty-five miles away. There she began to rebuild a life for herself.

With the help of Gerebernus, she devoted herself to the care of the needy and the forlorn. She rescued dozens of orphaned children from a life of begging in the streets. She gave shelter to the lame, the mentally impaired, and the infirm. She fearlessly lobbied for justice for the poor. And she fought to expose the dark secrets of abortionists whose flourishing contraband was wreaking havoc among the peasantry.

There in the Flemish lowlands, medievalism was progressively making its mark. The effects of Christian mercy had begun to permeate the culture just enough that the people had vaguely begun to recognize the notion that "Children are an heritage of the Lord; and the fruit of the womb is a reward from Him."

As a result, many of the most insidious practices from antiquity were passing from the scene—including the age old pagan procedures of infanticide, abandonment, and exposure. Even so, when there were serious problems with a pregnancy or when handicapped children were born, in desperation many families reverted to the pagan practices.

Dympna boldly challenged this, arguing that if human life is sacred, then all human life must be protected—regardless of how unlovely or inconvenient it might be. She sought to demonstrate that there was no such thing as an unwanted child.

Indeed, she acknowledged in deed what her faith enunciated in word, by making her home a haven for the otherwise unwanted. In the span of just three years, her household grew to include more than forty handicapped children and another twenty mentally impaired adolescents and adults.

Before long, she had gained a remarkable reputation for selflessness, graciousness, and charity. In the trying times of the eighth century, those were rare and welcome virtues. Barbarian hoards still threatened the frontier. Norse raiders terrorized the coastline. And petty feudal rivalries continued to paralyze the interior. After the fall of Rome in 476, Europe had lost its center of gravity and had become a spinning dreidel. Though Byzantium continued to flourish in the East, it was not until the slow but steady encroachment of medievalism covered the entire continent that any measure of peace or harmony could be secured.

The medieval period has commonly been called the Dark Ages—as if the light of civilization had been unceremoniously snuffed out. It has similarly been dubbed the Middle Ages—as if it were a gaping parenthesis in mankind's long upward march to modernity.

It was in fact anything but dark or middling. Perhaps our greatest fault is that we have limited ourselves by a parochialism in time. It is difficult for us to attribute anything but backwardness to those epochs and cultures that do not share our goals or aspirations.

The medieval period was actually quite remarkable for its many advances—perhaps unparalleled in all of history. It was a true nascence, while the epoch that followed was but a re-naissance. It was a new and living thing that gave flower to a culture marked by energy and creativity. From the monolithic security of Byzantium in the East to the reckless diversity of feuding fiefs in the West it was a glorious crazy quilt of human fabrics, textures, and hues.

Now to be sure, the medieval world was racked with abject poverty, ravaging plagues, and petty wars—much like our own day. It was haunted by superstition, prejudice, and corruption—as is the modern era. And it was beset by consuming ambition, perverse sin, and damnable folly—again, so like today. Still, it was free from the kind of crippling sophistication, insular ethnocentricity, and cosmopolitan provincialism that now shackle us—and so it was able to advance astonishingly.

The titanic innovations medievalism brought forth were legion: it gave birth to all the great universities of the world from Oxford and Cambridge to Leipzig to Mainz; it oversaw the establishment of all the great hospitals of the world from St. Bartholomew's and Bedlam in London to St. Bernard's and Voixanne in Switzerland; it brought forth the world's most celebrated artists from Michelangelo Buonarotti and Albrecht Durer to Leonardo da Vinci and Jan van Eyck; it gave us the splendor of Gothic architecture—unmatched and unmatchable to this day—from Notre Dame and Chartres to Winchester and Cologne; it thrust out into howling wilderness and storm tossed seas the most accomplished explorers from Amerigo Vespucci and Marco Polo to Vasco da Gama and Christopher Columbus; it produced some of the greatest minds and most fascinating lives mankind has yet known—were the list not so sterling it might begin to be tedious—Copernicus, Dante, Giotto, Becket, Gutenberg, Chaucer,

Charlemagne, Wyclif, Magellan, Botticelli, Donatello, Petrarch, and Aquinas.

But of all the great innovations that medievalism wrought, the greatest of all was spiritual. Medieval culture—both eastern and western—was first and foremost Christian culture. Its life was shaped almost entirely by Christian concerns. Virtually all of its achievements were submitted to the cause of the Gospel. From great cathedrals and gracious chivalry to long crusades and beautiful cloisters every manifestation of its presence was somehow tied to its utter and complete obeisance to Christ's kingdom.

Of course, the medieval church had its share of dangerous and scandalous behavior. It had gross libertines and rank heretics. It had false professors and bold opportunists. It had brutal ascetics and imbalanced tyrants. But then, there was no more of that sort of heterodoxy than we have today in Evangelical, Catholic, or Orthodox circles—and perhaps, considering recent headlines, a good deal less.

At any rate, spiritual concerns played a larger role in the lives of medieval men and women than at almost any other time before or since. And, as might be expected, that all-pervading interest was evidenced in a prominent concern for the protection of innocent life.

Dympna's work in Gheel—to say nothing of the testimony of her sterling character—offered tangible hope that the high aspirations of Christian civilization could be, and indeed would be, one day achieved. Thus, her work on behalf of the distressed was widely heralded.

Perhaps too widely.

Eadburh, upon hearing of his daughter's whereabouts, followed her to Gheel. There was an awful confrontation. When she refused to return home with him, he flew into a rage and brutally slew her.

Amazingly, Dympna's vision did not die with her that day. Stricken with sorrow, the citizens of Gheel decided to continue her mission of mercy. Her medieval ethic took root in their lives and became their work. Amazingly, that work continues to the present day—it includes a hospital for the mentally ill, a foundling center, an adoption agency, and the world's largest and most efficient boarding-out program for the afflicted and disturbed—run as a private and decentralized association by the Christian families of Gheel.

Interestingly, Dympna's heroics were matched by hundreds—perhaps even thousands—of others of equal valor and fruitfulness. A myriad of mercy ministries were founded throughout Europe during the medieval period—hospitals, orphanages, almshouses, charitable societies, relief agencies, hostels, and shelters. Monasteries opened their doors to oblate children, the unwanted who were given to the church. Towns and villages kept treasuries of alms gifts for the needy. The remnants of the old heathenism were driven out of the dark edges of the culture and out of existence.

The cause of the unloved and the unlovely—the ultimate lost cause—was taken up by those, like Dympna, who were able to both hear and heed the sweet strains of mercy.

All the starry hosts of heaven and of earth declare with one voice the glory bestowed on these sublime creatures of the Living God, these creatures made just a little lower than himself. We can do no better than to acknowledge our acceptance of Him by our acceptance of them.

Dympna of Gheel (c. 770–795)

Honor

*T*he very idea of risking our lives for the sake of honor seems
strangely absurd. We tend to be terribly practical—so much so that
we are willing to swallow all manner of indignity so as not to create
a furor. Compromise is our immediate response to the slings and
arrows of injustice. Honor is a veritable lost cause. But history is
filled to overflowing with examples of stalwart men and women
who believed that honor was the one thing that men and nations
must never be willing to exchange—not at any price; not for peace
or prosperity; not for comfort or contentment; not for appearance or
affluence. As a result, some of the greatest feats of valor
have been achieved for the simple sake of honor.

If I profess with the loudest voice and clearest exposition every portion of the truth of God except precisely that little point which the world and the devil are at the moment attacking, I am not confessing Christ, however boldly I may be professing Christ. Where the battle rages, there the loyalty of the soldier is proved, and to be steady on all the battle front besides, is mere flight and disgrace if he flinches at that point.

Martin Luther (1483–1546)

Knowing is not enough; we must apply. Understanding is not enough; we must do. Knowing and understanding in action make for honor. And honor is the heart of wisdom.

Johann von Goethe (1749–1832)

Better faithful than famous. Honor before prominence.

Theodore Roosevelt (1858–1919)

It was the pipes of the Highlanders,
And now they played Auld Lang Syne
It came to our men like the voice of God,
And they shouted along the line.
Robert Lowell (1816–1891)

Nothing is ended with honor which does not conclude better than it began.
Samuel Johnson (1709–1784)

There is no sacrifice I am not ready to make for the preservation of the Union save that of honor.
Robert E. Lee (1807–1870)

We make men without chests and expect of them virtue and enterprise. We laugh at honor and are shocked to find traitors in our midst. We castrate and bid the geldings be fruitful.
C. S. Lewis (1898–1963)

From the lowest place when virtuous things proceed,
The place is engulfed by the doer's deed:
When great additions swell, and virtue none,
It is a dropsied honor. As such,
mine honor is my life; both grow in one;
Take honor from me, and my life is done.

William Shakespeare (c. 1564–1616)

It is a greater honor to be right than to be president—or popular, for
statesmanship consists rather in removing causes than in punishing or evad-
ing results—thus, it is the rarest of qualities.

James A. Garfield (1831–1881)

Whether in slavery or in freedom, we have always conducted ourselves in
freedom—of such is the Negro's honor.

Booker T. Washington (1856–1915)

There is a true glory and a true honor; the glory of duty done—the honor
of the integrity of principle.

Robert E. Lee (1807–1870)

O, that estates, degrees, and offices,
Were not derived corruptly; and that clear honor
Were purchased by the merit of the wearer.
How many then should cover, that stand bare.
How many be commanded, that command.
How much low peasantry would then be gleaned
From the true seed of honor; and how much honor
Pick'd from the chaff of the times to be new varnished.

         William Shakespeare (c. 1564–1616)

Do your duty in all things. You cannot do more. You should never wish to do less.

         Robert E. Lee (1807–1870)

Better to die ten thousand deaths,
Than wound my honor.

         Joseph Addison (1672–1719)

If honor calls, where'er she points the way
The sons of honor follow, and obey.

         Winston Churchill (1874–1965)

The best things in life invariably cost us something. We must sacrifice to attain them, to achieve them, to keep them, even to enjoy them. That is one of the most important lessons we can learn in life. It is the message that we know we ought to instill in our children: patience, commitment, diligence, constancy, and discipline will ultimately pay off if we are willing to defer gratification long enough for the seeds we have sown to sprout and bear. A flippant, shallow, and imprecise approach to anything—be it sports or academics, business or pleasure, friendship or marriage—is ultimately self-defeating. It is not likely to satisfy any appetite—at least, not for long. The world is indeed full of seemingly harmless little distractions; humorous and silly things; banal and trivial things; things which take the path of least resistance; things which come cheaply and easily. Beware of all such things—they are the enemies of substance, truth, and honor.

Tristan Gylberd (1954–)

He that is valiant and dares fight,
Though drubbed, can lose no honor by't
Honor's a lease for lives to come,
And cannot be extended from
The legal tenant: 'tis a chattel
Not to be forfeited in battle.

Samuel Butler (1612–1680)

On the battlefield, when surrounded and cheered by pomp, excitement, and admiration of devoted comrades, and inspired by strains of martial music and the hope of future reward, it is comparatively easy to be a hero, to do heroic deeds. But to uphold honor in ordinary circumstances, to be a hero in common life, that is a genuine achievement meriting our highest admiration.

Booker T. Washington (1856–1915)

True conscious honor is to feel no sin:
He's armed without that's innocent within.

Alexander Pope (1688–1744)

The fear o' hell's a hangman's whip
To haud the wretch in order;
But where ye feel your honor grip,
Let that aye be your border.

Robert Burns (1759–1796)

His honor rooted in dishonor stood,
And faith unfaithful kept him falsely true.

Alfred, Lord Tennyson (1809–1892)

Speed bonnie boat, like a bird on the wing,
Onward the sailors cry!
Carry the lad that is born to be king,
Over the sea to Skye.

Loud the winds howl, loud the waves roar,
Thunder claps rend the air;
Baffled, our foes stand on the shore,
Follow, they will not dare.

Though the waves leap, soft shall yet sleep,
Ocean's a royal bed;
Rocked in the deep, Flora will keep
Watch by your weary head.

Many's the lad fought on that day,
Well the claymore could wield;
When the night came, silently lay
Dead on Culloden's field.

Burned are our homes, exile and death,
Scatter the honorable men;
Yet, e're the sword cool in the sheath,
Charlie will come again.

Lochiel MacEachain (1721–1794)

Bonnie Prince Charlie and the Legacy of Nobility

Determined to reclaim his family's inheritance, Bonnie Prince Charlie set out for his homeland of Scotland. His seven elderly companions—loyal courtiers of the expatriate royal—hardly constituted a fighting force. He had virtually no hope of attracting allies for his cause, he had no contacts in the land, he carried no money, and had no foreign support. He had no military experience, no weapons, and no clear plan. Nevertheless, he was committed to the legacy of his family, the justness of his claim, and the nobility of his charge.

His grandfather, James II, had been defeated by Parliamentary troops at the Battle of the Boyne sealed the Great Revolution of 1688 and deposed the Stuart monarchy of Great Britain. Living in exile in France, the family pressed its claim against the Hanoverian usurpers again and again over the next seventy years—but all to no avail. The British repeatedly repulsed the royal family and its loyal subjects so that the hope of a Stuart restoration increasingly became little more than a romantic lost cause.

Resigned to his restless exile, the prince's father, James III, was a morose and defeated man. As a result Bonnie Prince Charlie grew up in a hopeless environment of despair. But somehow he was never infected with that sense of futility and finality. He held on to the dream that one day his family might again reign supreme in London and Edinburgh—as was their due. His princely qualities—and deep devotion to his family's rich legacy of nobility—were evident to all.

In 1745, at the age of twenty-five, he determined that he must attempt to recover his father's inheritance. And so he set out on his quixotic journey.

At first, the landlords, nobles, and lairds he met scoffed at the idea that the long-deposed Stuarts might be able to mount a legitimate claim for the throne. The Hanoverians and Parliamentarians controlled the greatest military force on the face of the earth. They commanded the world's largest treasury. And the citizens were enjoying an unprecedented season of peace and prosperity. Such conditions hardly bode well for a penniless, directionless, grassroots insurgency.

But the young prince would not be deterred. And his utter sincerity, his courageous bearing, his inspiring devotion, and his articulate oratory made believers out of nearly everyone he came into contact with. Traversing from cotter village to clan castle and from loch settlement to noble palace, he began to attract the attentions and command the loyalties of the stalwart Highlanders. He went from the outer Hebrides in the far west to the heart of the country at Glenaladale. There with his wild and untamed partisans around him—tartans blazing, bagpipes wailing, and chieftans shouting—he raised the standard of the Stuarts.

His father was proclaimed king and the prince was named the regent. A national covenant—a kind of spiritual and political manifesto—lamented the fact that Scotland had been reduced to the condition of a province, under the specious pretense of union with England. The prince then declared a general pardon, guaranteed a free parliament and religious freedom, and promised to advance trade, relieve the poor, and establish the general welfare and tranquility of the nation. Cheers filled the glen—and an insurgency was launched. A few weeks later, he marched triumphantly into Edinburgh.

His armed band grew with every passing day. Eventually, he was forced to face the military might of the Hanovarians who were becoming increasingly alarmed by the unexpected turn of events in their northern province. Along the borders of Northumbria at the field of Prestonpans, the young prince engineered a stunning victory over the vastly better equipped English. The trained British troops were simply unprepared to face the unfettered fury and untempered loyalty of the Highlanders.

After a series of other minor field victories, the prince ordered his troops toward London in the south. In one stunning maneuver after another, he outwitted the English commanders and was able to eventually control more than three-quarters of the land. He came within fifty miles of London. The Hanoverian king, George II, was in a panic, making haste to leave for his German homeland.

It was treachery that eventually turned Bonnie Prince Charlie back, spoiling his fairy tale aspirations. Betrayed by several of his nobles, he was forced to retreat back toward Scotland. The English armies, taking advantage of this turn of events, pursued with all haste. Over the next several months, the Highlanders were harried by both their enemies and the weather.

Though they were able to prevail in several of the skirmishes and battles that followed—including the decisive Battle of Falkirk—by the winter of 1746, it was clear that the Hanoverians had taken the upper hand. The prince and his men were on the defensive.

The final pitched battle between the two forces took place on Culloden Moor just outside Inverness, in the far northern reaches of the Scottish Highlands. The calamitous slaughter took less than half an hour. The well-equipped Hanoverian troops swept over the field and exacted the horrible price of vengeance. The prince escaped with his life, but little else. Over the next five months Bonnie Prince Charlie wandered as a fugitive in the Highlands while the Hanoverians ravaged Scotland, raping and pillaging their way across the whole land. The Scottish tongue, Gaelic, was banned, as were all the distinctive aspects of Scots culture—from bagpipes and kilts to tartans and clan badges. Alas, the prince could do little to ameliorate the suffering of his people.

Eventually, he was able to steal away into exile, where he spent the rest of his life. He never gave up on the Stuart cause though. He maintained his claims. And his descendants to this very day claim the royal prerogative.

Of course, such a claim has always sounded rather hollow in the face of the British royal family's stranglehold on the public's attention. And besides, the universal infatuation with democratic republicanism has made any talk of monarchical standards seem little more than quaint in these modern times.

Nevertheless, there is something very attractive about the bravery, loyalty, and noble bearing of Bonnie Prince Charlie that continues to attract the affections of men and nations. And with the return of parliamentary independence for Scotland, there is renewed interest in the Stuart claims of the current Prince Michael. As in Russia where there has been a revival of the Romanov fortunes, in Austria where the Hapsburgs are once again prominently featured in political discussions, and in Germany where the Hohenzollerns and Hohenstaufens are once again claiming the attentions of the people, concern for royal prerogatives is not so much a matter of genealogy, land, and privilege as it is of nobility, justice, and dignity. As at no other time in recent memory, men and nations are yearning for the kind of glory Western civilization offered in days gone by—a glory whose stewardship was entrusted to guardians of tradition like Bonnie Prince Charlie.

The reality is that such a legacy has forever been an alluring paradox. It has been a romantic riddle. On the one hand it was marked by the greatest virtues of morality, charity, and selflessness; on the other hand it was marred by the flaming vices of perversity, betrayal, and avarice. It was often timid, monkish, and isolated; oftener still, it was bold, ostentatious, and adventurous. It was mystical; it was worldly. It was tender-hearted; it was cruel. It was ascetic; it was sensual. It was miserly; it was pretentious. It gripped men with a morbid superstition; it set them free with an untamed inquisitiveness. It exulted in pomp, circumstance, and ceremony; it cowered in poverty, tyranny, and injustice. It united men with faith, hope, and love; it divided them with war, pestilence, and prejudice. It was so unstable it could hardly have been expected to last a week; it was so stable that it actually lasted a millenium.

The contrast with modern culture is stark. The contrast is stark precisely because men like Bonnie Prince Charlie actually lived out—however imperfectly—the implications of the world-view of Christendom. Now, whenever the subject of world-view comes up, we moderns typically think of philosophy. And that is really too bad. We think of intellectual niggling. We think of theological lint picking. We think of the brief and blinding oblivion of ivory tower speculation, of thickly obscure tomes, and of inscrutable logical complexities. In fact, a world-view is as practical as garden arbors, public manners, whistling at work, dinnertime rituals, and architectural angels. It is less metaphysical than understanding marginal market buying at the stock exchange or legislative initiatives in Congress. It is less esoteric than typing a book into a laptop computer or sending a fax across the continent. It is instead, as down to earth as inculcating a culture-wide appetite for beauty, truth, and goodness.

That is precisely what Bonnie Price Charlie was fighting for. And as a result, his was anything but a lost cause.

The legacy of nobility, which is at the heart of the royal Stuart claim, is the great cause of all men who are friends of liberty, of truth, of civilization.

Bonnie Prince Charlie (1720–1788)

Chivalry

*M*ention chivalry and most of us are apt to think of knights in shining armor, damsels in distress, crusaders embarking on a great challenge, or pilgrims intent on a pious quest. It is a rather romantic notion that brings to mind Arthur and his Round Table, Ivanhoe and his lost honor, Guinevere and her threatened virtue, and Rapunsel and her dire straits. It evokes images of the long ago and the far away. It is, for us, rather passé. It is a positively medieval concept—a long forgotten relic of the sentimental past. But chivalry is a code of honorable conduct that needs not necessarily be tied to any particular time or place or cultural context. As wise men and women throughout all time have known, it is a standard of virtuous behavior that has inspired great men and women through all the ages— causing them to long for a kinder, gentler society that abides by the conditions of genuine civilization.

Chivalry gives naught but itself and takes naught but from itself. Chivalry possesses not nor would it be possessed—for it is sufficient unto love.

James Villars (1891–1973)

The age of chivalry is gone, alas; that of sophisters, economists, and calculators has succeeded.

Edmund Burke (1729–1797)

It is to be steadily inculcated, that virtue is the highest proof of understanding, and the only solid basis of greatness.

Samuel Johnson (1709–1784)

Thou knowest not how impossible it is for one trained to actions of chivalry to remain passive as a priest, or a woman, when they are acting deeds of honour around him. The love of battle is the food upon which we live—the dust of the melee is the breath of our nostrils! We live not—we wish not to live—longer than while we are victorious and renowned. Such, maiden, are the laws of chivalry to which we are sworn, and to which we offer all that we hold dear.

Sir Walter Scott (1771–1832)

Chivalry is knowing what to do in a given situation and then having the courage to act without regard to the outcome.

Rex Page (1952–)

The funeral sermon of the chivalry of Christendom and the old South has been preached so many times that most people probably thought it was really going to be interred. But horrific inhumanity of modernity's humanism has served as a kind of benevolent cataclysm which shattered the smothering uniformity of contemporary barbarism, and once again, it seems, civilization may be seen as an option by thinking men and women. Ever hopeful, the phoenix of chivalry may yet rise from the ashes of this misbegotten wreckage we call modern pop culture.

Tristan Gylberd (1954–)

The Christian and the hero are inseparable—chiefly because of the effects of chivalry upon the character.

Samuel Johnson (1709–1784)

So to be patriots as not to forget we are gentlemen.

Edmund Burke (1729–1797)

Oh! Those blessed times of old!
With their chivalry and state;
I love to read their chronicles,
Which such brave deeds relate;
I love to sing their ancient rhymes,
To hear their legends told.

Frances Brown (1816–1864)

Chivalry is the ideal code of ethical behavior—ultimately based on scripture—that defines the limits of proper action toward other people.

Rex Page (1952–)

We must diligently strive to make our young men decent, God-fearing, law-abiding, honor-loving, justice-doing, and also fearless and strong, able to hold their own in the hurly-burly of the world's work, able to strive mightily that the forces of right may be in the end triumphant. And we must be ever vigilant in so telling them.

Theodore Roosevelt (1858–1919)

Young gentlemen, we have no printed rules. We have but one rule here, and it is that every one of you must be a Christian gentleman.

Robert E. Lee (1807–1870)

The old South preserved the last vestiges of chivalry in this poor fallen world. Thus, to long for the return of its manners, customs, and mores—indeed, for a return of its civilization—is hardly the impulse of sentiment, prejudice, or nostalgia. Instead, it is the rational yearning of Christian affection.

Robert Penn Warren (1905–1989)

And I heard above bannerets blown the intolerant trumpets of honor, that usher with iron laughter the coming of Christian arms.

G. K. Chesterton (1874–1936)

Life is not so short but that there is always time enough for courtesy and chivalry.

Ralph Waldo Emerson (1803–1882)

Zealous, yet modest; innocent, though free; Patient of toil, serene amidst alarms; Inflexible in faith, invincible in arms.

ᛂ James Beattie (1735–1803) ᛂ

There is no outward sign of true chivalry that does not rest on a deep moral foundation.

ᛂ Johann Goethe (1749–1832) ᛂ

Amor vincit omnia.

ᛂ Geoffrey Chaucer (1343–1400) ᛂ

The browning honey-horns droop and faint,
Exhale in rainbow drops a timorous essence,
And spend their whiff of fragrance all unheeded
On lustful winds who whirl far to the South
Heated with expectation of lying that night
On the voluptuous breast of weeping willow,
Flowing its hair beside some moon-lit river.

ᛂ Andrew Nelson Lytle (1902–1995) ᛂ

When the pale of chivalry is broken, rudeness and insult soon enter the breach.

Samuel Johnson (1709–1784)

The unbought grace of life, the cheap defense of nations, the nurse of manly sentiment, and the heroic enterprise is lost to us in all but the hearts of romantic visionaries and poets. Lament for the lost cause of chivalry.

Edmund Burke (1729–1797)

Such is chivalry:
Off goes his bonnet to an oyster wench.

William Shakespeare (c. 1564–1616)

And when you know a lady's in the case,
The chivalrous man the a'set,
You know all other things give place,
And thus the qualms of honor met.

John Gay (1685–1732)

Ne'er was flattery lost on a poet's ear:
A simple race. They waste their toil
For the vain tribute of a smile;
While knights bound by chivalry hear
The call of hope, help, and soil,
For the glory of but the honorable phile.

Sir Walter Scott (1771–1832)

ANDREW NELSON LYTLE AND THE HUNGER FOR SOUTHERN GENTILITY

He was just twenty-eight years old when he joined an extraordinary group of Southern historians, poets, political scientists, novelists, and journalists in publishing a prophetic collection of essays warning against the looming loss of the original vision of American life—a vision of both liberty and virtue. The symposium—entitled *I'll Take My Stand*—poignantly voiced the complex intellectual, emotional, and spiritual consternation of men standing on the precipice of catastrophic cultural change. Andrew Nelson Lytle was still a graduate student at Vanderbilt University in 1930, but already he was recognized by the literary luminaries that made up the group—such notables as Robert Penn Warren, Donald Davidson, Allen Tate, Stark Young, and John Crowe Ransom—as a brilliant writer and a wise exponent of their philosophy of chivalry, stability, and agrarian virtue.

The Agrarians—as the group came to be called—were alarmed by what they perceived to be a steady erosion of the rule of law in modern American life. They feared that—as was the case in the eighteenth century—our liberties were facing a fearsome challenge from the almost omnipresent and omnipotent forces of monolithic government. They said, "When we remember the high expectations held universally by the founders of the American union for a more perfect order of society, and then consider the state of life in this country today, it is bound to appear to reasonable people that somehow the experiment has very nearly proved abortive, and that in some way a great commonwealth has gone wrong."

They were determined to warn against the creeping dehumanization of an ideological secularism that they believed was already beginning to dominate American life. "There is evidently a kind of thinking that rejoices in setting up a social objective which has no relation to the individual. Men are prepared to sacrifice their private dignity and happiness to an abstract social ideal, and without asking whether the social ideal produces the welfare of any individual man whatsoever."

Lytle, like the other Agrarians, was the product of the post-Reconstruction era in the South. It was a difficult time in a difficult place. The virtues of Southern gentility, though sorely tested since the time of the War Between the States and its horrendous aftermath, were still very much in evidence. Despite the region's captivity to the economic and cultural domination of the North, the old principles and precepts survived. Indeed, in some quarters—such as the classical academic environment of the Vanderbilt campus—they actually thrived.

He was born in 1902, into a family with deep roots in both the soil and the society of the Old South. He was reared on a rich diet of family closeness, hard work in the fields, community cohesiveness, deep piety, and a legacy of storytelling that would ever afterward shape his vision of the good life. He loved the culture of the South for all its genuineness, its traditionalism, and its humaneness.

But of course Lytle knew full well that he, his Agrarian cohorts, and all the other advocates of that residual Southern civilization were essentially standing against the rising tide of industrial modernity. Nevertheless, he was convinced that ordinary Americans would ultimately hear and heed their warning—otherwise, the nation would collapse under the weight of corruption. The Agrarians sounded the alarm: "If the republic is to live up to its ideals and be what it could be, then it had better look long and hard at what it is in danger of becoming and devote conscious effort to controlling its own destiny, rather than continuing to drift along on the tides of economic materialism."

Clearly, all of the Agrarians were old-line conservatives in the tradition of Americans like John Adams, Fisher Ames, John Randolph, and John Calhoun. But they also drew on the rich European conservative tradition of men like Edmund Burke, Walter Bagehot, Robert Southey, and Thomas Macaulay. As political scientist Louis Rubin later commented, "They were writing squarely out of an old American tradition, one that we find imbedded in American thought almost from the earliest days. The tradition was that of the pastorale; they were invoking the humane virtues of a simpler, more elemental, non-acquisitive existence, as a needed rebuke to the acquisitive, essentially materialistic compulsions of a society that from the outset was very much engaged in seeking wealth, power, and plenty on a continent whose prolific natural resources and vast acres of usable land, forests, and rivers were there for the taking."

Short-term pessimists but long-term optimists, they believed that eventually a grassroots movement would restore the principles of the rule of law and that the American dream could be preserved for future generations. Though they were not economists or sociologists or activists, their vision was a comprehensive blueprint for a genuinely principle-based conservative renewal.

Thus they believed in an extremely limited form of government and took a dim view of government intervention. They went so far as to assert that communities should "ask practically nothing of the federal government in domestic legislation." Further, they believed that this limited governmental structure should be predicated primarily on the tenets of "local self-government" and "decentralization."

They were not minimalists or libertarians. Instead they were realists who envisioned a society which called "only for enough government to prevent men from injuring one another." It was by its very nature a "non-ideological" and "*laissez-faire* society." It was an "individualistic society" that "only asked to be let alone."

Not surprisingly then, the contributors to the symposium opposed the idea that "the government should set up an economic super organization, which in turn would become the government." They regarded socialism, democratic liberalism, communism, and republican cooperationism with equal disdain. In fact, they professed an ingrained "suspicion of all schemes that propose to coerce our people to their alleged benefit."

They believed that it was necessary "to employ a certain skepticism even at the expense of the Cult of Science, and to say it is an Americanism, which looks innocent and disinterested, but really is not either." They were not resistant to technological progress so much as they were resistant to the crass and inhuman humanism that often accompanies industrial advance. They believed that "a way of life that omits or de-emphasizes the more spiritual side of existence is necessarily disastrous to all phases of life."

Clearly then, the Agrarians who contributed to *I'll Take My Stand* believed that society ought to be defined by its moral and cultural values. They yearned for return to that early American ethic of freedom and liberty that was "for the most part stable, religious, and agrarian; where the goodness of life was measured by a scale of values having little to do with material values."

In essence, they believed in humanizing the scale of modern life: "restoring such practices as manners, conversation, hospitality, sympathy, family life, romantic love—the social exchanges which reveal and develop sensibility in human affairs." They believed in a "realistic, stable, and hereditable life." Thus they favored continuity and tradition over change for the sake of change: "The past is always a rebuke to the present; it's a better rebuke than any dream of the future. It's a better rebuke because you can see what some of the costs were, what frail virtues were achieved in the past by frail men." After all, they said, "Affections, and long memories, attach to the ancient bowers of life in the provinces; but they will not attach to what is always changing."

Although they believed that all of these foundational truths were "self-evident" in the sense that they are written on the fleshly tablet of every man's heart, they were not so idealistic as to believe that the truths would be universally accepted. In fact, they knew that such reasoning would inevitably be a stumbling block to some and mere foolishness to others. All too often men suppress reality in one way, shape, form, or another.

As a matter of fact, though *I'll Take My Stand* caused quite a stir when it was first released, very few critics gave it much chance of actually affecting the course of events or the destiny of the nation. It was assumed that "the wheels of progress could not possibly be redirected." The contributors were chided for their "naiveté," "impracticality," and "idealism." They were written off as "merely nostalgic," "hopelessly utopian," and "enthusiasts for an epochal past that can never again be recaptured."

For some fifty years it looked as if the critics might be right. The course of the twentieth century appeared to be a stern rebuke to the basic principles of the symposium. Like the English Distributists and the Continental Christian Democrats, with whom they shared so many basic presuppositions, the Agrarians seemed tragically out of step with the times. Their commitment to the old standards of chivalry seemed to be a hopelessly lost cause.

But now all that has changed. Recent turns of events have vindicated their emphasis on less government, lower taxes, family values, minimal regulation, and localism. Their innate distrust of professional politicians, propagandizing media, and commercial tomfoolery have suddenly been translated by a spontaneous grassroots advent into populist megatrends. The fulfillment of their improbable prophetic caveat is even now unfolding as we race toward the end of the century.

Lytle actually lived to see the genesis of the cultural about-face. His long career as a gentleman farmer, novelist, essayist, university professor, and writing mentor earned him a tenured place among Southern *belles lettres*. His log cabin on Monteagle became a gathering place for a kind of cultural expatriate movement. His chivalrous demeanor and his venerable mien became for generations of young Southern writers the very embodiment of the social and spiritual ideal. At his death in 1995, he was lauded as a prophet—not of a way of life now long gone, but of a hope merely deferred.

Engendering a common sense of gentility, that great Southern grace, ought to be the object of every chivalrous artist—writer, musician, painter, sculptor, performer, and architect—lest the best of our civilization escape from the modern world altogether.

Andrew Nelson Lytle (1902–1995)

Courage

*T*hough we tend to admire courage, we often have to admit that there is an unexplainable admixture of boldness and madness in it. Concerned with our own health and welfare, we find it more than a little extraordinary when anyone is willing to risk life and limb for the sake of others—much less for the sake of some principle. Indeed, we have become an age with a dearth of heroes. Bravery has practically become a forgotten virtue—a lost cause. Nevertheless, its allure retains as strong a grip on us today as it has each of the many generations that have preceded us.

Any coward can fight a battle when he's sure of winning; but give me the man who has the pluck to fight when he's sure of losing. That's my way, sir; and there are many victories worse than a defeat.

George Eliot (1819–1880)

Fear can keep a man out of danger, but courage can support him in it.

Thomas Fuller (1608–1661)

Have courage for the great sorrows of life and patience for the small ones. And when you have laboriously accomplished your daily task, go to sleep in peace. God is awake.

Victor Hugo (1802–1885)

If you want courage in any disaster,
Carefully constantly follow the Master.
There's no discouragement
That can make you relent

Your promise, your intent, to be a pilgrim.

When people tell you you're fighting a lost war,
They just confuse themselves; your strength will grow more.
You are God's chosen knight;
Though with you giants fight.

You will make good your right to be a pilgrim.

Since God Himself defends us with His Spirit
He guarantees the new life we inherit.
Lingering doubts fly away!
No matter what you say!

I'll labor night and day to be a pilgrim.

John Bunyan (1628–1688)

No coward soul is mine,
No trembler in the world's storm-troubled sphere:
I see Heaven's glories shine,
And faith shines equal, arming me from fear.

Emily Brontë (1818–1848)

The world has no room for cowards. We must all be ready somehow to toil, to suffer, to die. And yours is not the less noble because no drum beats before you when you go out into your daily battlefields, and no crowds shout about your coming when you return from your daily victory or defeat.

Robert Lewis Stevenson (1850–1894)

In valor there is hope.

Tacitus (c. 55–120)

If all the world were just, there would be no need of valor.

Plutarch (c. 49–120)

We cannot expect a more cordial welcome than disturbers of complacency have received in any other age.

Richard Weaver (1910–1963)

Courage is not having the strength to go on; it is going on when you don't have the strength. Industry and determination can do anything that genius and advantage can do and many things that they cannot.

Theodore Roosevelt (1858–1919)

He has not learned the lesson of life who does not every day surmount a fear.

Ralph Waldo Emerson (1803–1882)

A mighty fortress is our God,
A bulwark never failing;
Our helper He amid the flood
Of mortal ills prevailing.
For still our ancient foe
Doth seek to work us woe;
His craft and power are great;
And armed with cruel hate,
On earth is not his equal.

And though this world, with devils filled,
Should threaten to undo us,
We will not fear, for God hath willed
His truth to triumph through us.
The prince of darkness grim,
We tremble not for him;
His rage we can endure,
For, lo, his doom is sure;
One little word shall fell him.

Martin Luther (1483–1546)

Cowards die many times before their deaths;
The valiant never taste of death but once.
William Shakespeare (c. 1564–1616)

Courage is almost a contradiction in terms. It means a strong desire to live taking the form of a readiness to die.
G. K. Chesterton (1874–1936)

Where courage is not, no other virtue can survive except by accident.
Samuel Johnson (1709–1784)

One man with courage makes a majority.
Andrew Jackson (1767–1845)

The only thing we have to fear is fear itself.
Franklin Delano Roosevelt (1882–1945)

If we take the generally accepted definition of bravery as a quality which knows not fear, I have never seen a brave man. All men are frightened. The more intelligent they are, the more they are frightened. The courageous man is the man who forces himself, in spite of his fear, to carry on.

General George Patton (1885–1945)

Let liars fear, let cowards shrink,
Let traitors turn away,
Whatever we have dared to think
That we dare to say.

James Russell Lowell (1819–1891)

The fear of God makes a hero; the fear of man makes a coward.

Alvin York (1887–1964)

Tell a man he is brave, and you help him to become so.
Thomas Carlyle (1795–1881)

Courage is what it takes to stand up and speak; courage is also what it takes to sit down and listen.
Winston Churchill (1874–1965)

Courage is grace under pressure.
Ernest Hemingway (1899–1961)

To see what is right and not to do it is cowardice. It is never a question of who is right but what is right.
John Buchan (1875–1940)

I am of certain convinced that the greatest heroes are those who do their duty in the daily grind of domestic affairs whilst the world whirls as a maddening dreidel.

ᴏᵻ *Florence Nightengale (1820–1910)* ᵻᴏ

Courage consists not in hazarding without fear, but being resolutely minded in a just cause.

ᴏᵻ *Plutarch (c. 49–120)* ᵻᴏ

Courage: the footstool of the virtues, upon which they stand.

ᴏᵻ *Robert Louis Stevenson (1850–1894)* ᵻᴏ

If a thing is worth doing, it is worth doing badly.

ᴏᵻ *G. K. Chesterton (1874–1936)* ᵻᴏ

The courage we desire and prize is not the courage to die decently but to live manfully.

Thomas Carlyle (1795–1881)

Courage is resistance to fear, mastery of fear—not absence of fear. Except a creature be part coward, it is not a compliment to say it is brave.

Mark Twain (1835–1910)

Brethren, standfast.

Paul of Tarsus (c. 10–65)

Courage and resolution are the spirit and soul of virtue.

Thomas Fuller (1608–1661)

Without belittling the courage with which men have died, we should not forget those acts of courage with which men have lived. The courage of life is often a less dramatic spectacle than the courage of a final moment; but it is no less a magnificent mixture of triumph and tragedy. A man does what he must—in spite of personal consequences and dangers and pressures— and that is the basis of all human morality. In whatever arena of life one may meet the challenge of courage, whatever may be the sacrifices he faces if he follows his conscience—the loss of his friends, his fortune, his contentment, even the esteem of his fellow men—each man must decide for himself the course he will follow. The stories of past courage can define that ingredient—they can teach, they can offer hope, they can provide inspiration. But they cannot supply courage itself. For this each man must look into his own soul.

John F. Kennedy (1917–1963)

A man should stop his ears against paralyzing terror, and run the race that is set before him with a single mind.

Robert Louis Stevenson (1850–1894)

Courage is a character trait most oft attributable to men. In fact, it is the universal virtue of all those who choose to do the right thing over the expedient thing. It is the common currency of all those who do what they are supposed to do in a time of conflict, crisis, and confusion.

Florence Nightengale (1820–1910)

Real valor consists not in being insensible to danger, but in being prompt to confront and disarm it.

Sir Walter Scott (1771–1832)

There is little extraordinary about the achievements of a genius, a prodigy, or a savant. Inevitably, a great leader is someone who overcomes tremendous obstacles and still succeeds. That is the essence of courage. It is the ability to maintain, in the face of grave perils, a kind of incognizance of the consequences of doing right. It is the ability to maintain great strength without any impulsive compulsion to use it—that strength is to be held in reserve until and unless it becomes necessary to use it for the cause of right.

Tristan Gylberd (1954–)

Courage is not simply one of the virtues, but the form of every virtue at the testing point, which means, at the point of highest reality. A chastity or honesty or mercy which yields to danger will be chaste or honest or merciful only on conditions. Pilate was merciful until it became risky.

C. S. Lewis (1898–1963)

Anna Bowden and the Cause of Justice

India in the nineteenth century was no place for a lady—or at least, it was no place for an impressionable young lady, born and bred in the comfort and ease of Victorian England. It was a rough and tumble world of stark brutality and crass occultism. It was a chaotic and untamed spiritual Negev.

The bestial cult of Kali enslaved millions in wretched fear and perversity. The cruel and impersonal rigors of Brahmanism racked millions more with the fickle whims of fashion and fancy. Still more were gripped in the bizarre downward spiral of fatalistic self-abasement, inhuman social stratification, and raw moral corruption of Vedacism. And besides these divergent branches of Hinduism, a jangling kaleidoscope of competing cosmic visions—Moslem, Sikh, and Buddhist—imposed on the great Asian subcontinent a nasty paganism of anarchy and unrest.

Anna Bowden was a consummate Victorian debutante. She was a lady. But she burst fearlessly onto that awful cultural landscape with faith, hope, and love.

With a remarkable singleness of heart and soul, Anna left her family's comfortable Notting Hill social orbit of staid and privatistic Anglicanism to enroll in Henrietta Soltau's mission training school in London. Formed as an adjunct to the work of J. Hudson Taylor's China Inland Mission, the school provided candidate screening and intensive preparation for women who had yielded to the call of foreign missionary work.

Late in 1891 Robert Campbell-Green, an itinerant evangelist working in southern India, visited the school to deliver a short series of devotional talks on the many new missionary inroads that he had recently witnessed in the Mysore, Madras, and Pradesh provinces. He related the brutal realities of the dominant Hindu culture—the awful disrespect of the poor, the weak, the helpless, and the low-born as well as the spiritual captivity to dark and damning passions. Anna was completely mesmerized. She felt an irresistible call to take the message of the Gospel and the succor of Christ to that desperate land. Though only midway through her training, she immediately—almost impulsively—committed herself to the fledgling work there. A month later, she set sail for Conjeeveram.

Her idealistic travel journal conveys the overriding vision that she carried into the work, "I know not the challenges that face me among peoples who live but for death. I do know though, the grace of the Savior that has called me to die but for life."

When she arrived in Conjeeveram—a seacoast town about twenty-five miles north of Kanchipuram and about forty miles south of Madras—she discovered that the mission compound of Campbell-Green had been abandoned. Apparently, there was nothing to indicate what had happened or where the missionaries had gone. The only other English residents in the region—a small community of fabric exporters—could say only that the mission had been vacant for quite some time and that the residents of the compound had suddenly disappeared without a trace.

Despite this staggering turn of events, Anna remained undeterred. Working with the occasional and begrudging aid of the English merchants, she refurbished the mission's decrepit facilities and reopened its tiny clinic and school.

Although most of the local residents generally maintained a cool distance, Anna's tender and magnetic personality drew innumerable children and outcaste "untouchables" into her circle. After only three months, her solitary efforts began to reap a bountiful harvest.

It was not long, however, before Anna's jubilant optimism ran headlong into trouble. A fairly new Hindu reform movement had begun to spread in southern India—the Arya Samaj. Dedicated to the purification of Hinduism and a return to the traditional values of ancient paganism, the adherents of Arya Samaj were bitterly anti-Western and anti-Christian. They sought a ban on "proselytism" and reinstituted such practices as immolation and *sarti*—the ritual sacrifice of widows on the funeral biers of their husbands—as well as *deyana*—female infanticide—and *kananda*—cultic abortifacient procedures. Although a number of very prominent missionaries attempted to adhere to the longstanding British colonial policy of noninterference—including William Miller, the renowned principal of the nearby Christian College of Madras—Anna simply could not stand idly by while the innocents were slaughtered. She immediately set up a rescue network—providing ready escape for damned widows. And she pulled together a cadre of committed believers to interfere with the practices and procedures of the infanticide guilds.

Describing her motivation for such drastic and dramatic activities, she wrote: "The mandate of Holy Writ is plain. We must clothe the naked, feed the hungry, shelter the shelterless, succor the infirmed, and rescue the perishing. I can do no less and still be faithful to the high call of our Sovereign Lord."

Apparently, her crusade began to exact a toll on the traditionalist Hindu movement because early in 1893, Swami Dayanand Sarasvati, the leader of Arya Samaj, appealed to Queen Victoria's viceroy to have Anna stopped. In an attempt to keep the peace, the British administrator ordered Anna to refrain from any activities that were not "directly related to the operation of the missionary outpost." Anna replied saying that rescuing innocent human life was indeed "directly related" to her mission work and that in fact, it was "directly related to any form of Christian endeavor, humanitarian or evangelistic."

Impatient and dissatisfied with the viceroy's meek handling of Anna, Sarasvati dispatched an angry mob of his followers to the mission compound. They burned several of the buildings to the ground, raped a number of the young girls who had come to live there, and tortured and killed Anna.

The accession of the Christian culture of Europe as the world's dominating socio-political force was actually not assured until well into the nineteenth century. In fact, for the bulk of its first two millennia Christian culture had been strikingly unsuccessful in spreading its estimable effects beyond European shores. In the Far East, for instance, missionary endeavors were practically nonexistent in China and paralyzed by persecution in Japan. In India the higher castes were virtually untouched by the Gospel, and even the lower castes showed only transitory interest. The Islamic lands were as resistant as always to the inroads of the church. South America's conversion to the conquistador's Catholicism was tenuous at best. And tropical Africa had proven to be so formidable and inhospitable that Western settlements were confined to a few small outposts along the coast. Clearly, Christianity was still very much a white man's religion.

There had been, of course, a few bursts of expansion. In 1453, a series of catastrophic events—both good and bad—freed European monarchs to cast their vision outward for the first time since the early crusades. That year saw the defeat of Constantine XI by Sultan Mohammed II—thus bringing an end to the storied Byzantine Empire. In addition, the Hundred Years War between England and France ended, as did wars between Venice and Milan, Russia and Lithuania, and Prussia and Poland. The Habsburgs and the Medicis were both bolstered in their respective realms. And Guttenberg's press in Mainz altered the transmission of knowledge and culture forever with the publication of the first printed book—a Bible.

Explorers had begun to venture out into uncharted realms. Scientists began to probe long hidden mysteries. Traders and merchants started carving out new routes, new markets, and new technologies. Energies that had previously been devoted exclusively to survival were redirected by local magistrates into projects and programs designed to improve health, hygiene, and the common good. Africa, India, China, Indonesia, and the Americas were soon opened to exploration and exploitation. From colonial outposts there, a tremendous wealth of exotic raw resources poured into European cities.

But despite all these advantages, European advances were limited and short lived—and the Gospel made only halting and sporadic progress. Internecine warfare and petty territorialism disrupted—and very nearly nullified—even that much Christian influence. From 1688—when William and Mary concluded the Glorious Revolution in England by ascending to the throne, Louis XIV canonized the iron-fisted notion of "Divine Right," and young Peter Romanov became czar of all the Russias—until 1848—when the calamitous Marxist rebellions in Paris, Rome, Venice, Berlin, Parma, Vienna, and Milan were finally squelched—Europe was racked by one convulsive struggle after another. During those two centuries, the cause of Christian unity, veracity, and temerity was wore a Khazar face—buffeted by the Austro-Prussian wars, the Napoleonic wars, the American War of Independence, the Persian-Ottoman wars, the Sino-Russian wars, the French Revolution, the Greek and the South American wars of independence, and the Mogul invasions. The entire culture seemed to be driven by an Arimathean impulse to bury disparaged truth.

At last though, a hush of peace fell upon the continent during the Victorian Age, a Pax Britannia. And within the span of a generation, the message of Christ and the benefits of a Christian culture and law code were impressed upon the whole earth.

Three great revolutions—beginning first in England and then spreading throughout all the European dominions—laid the foundations for this remarkable turn of events. The first was the Agricultural Revolution. The replacement of fallowing with leguminous rotation, the use of chemical fertilizers, and the introduction of farm machinery enabled Europeans to virtually break the cycle of famine and triage across the continent for the first time in mankind's history. The second was the Industrial Revolution. Manufactured goods and the division of labor created a broad-based middle class and freed the unlanded masses—again, for the first time in human history. The third was the Transportation Revolution. At the beginning of the nineteenth century, Napoleon could not cross his domain any more efficiently than Nebuchadnezzar could have crossed his six centuries before Christ. By the end of the Victorian age, men were racing across the rails and roads in motorized vehicles of stupendous power, they were crashing over and under the waves of the sea in iron vessels of enormous size, and they were cutting through the clouds in ingenious zeppelins, balloons, and gliders.

The earth had become a European planet. Whole continents were carved up between the rival monarchs. With a thrashing overheated quality—in which charity and good sense are sometimes sacrificed for the practical end of beating the Hun—Africa, Asia, Australia, the Far East, Latin America, and the Middle East became the backyard playgrounds of speculative colonists and imperial opportunists.

Just as no corner of the globe was left untouched by the explorers, soldiers, merchants, and colonists bearing up under notions of the "White Man's Burden" and "Manifest Destiny," the selfless and sacrificial efforts of missionaries left virtually no stone unturned either. Peoples everywhere tasted their abundant benefits. And chief among those benefits, of course, was a new respect for innocent human life—a respect that was entirely unknown anywhere in the world until the advent of the Gospel.

As missionaries moved out from Christendom to the "uttermost parts of the earth" they were shocked to discover all the horrors of untamed heathenism. They found infanticide all too commonplace, abandonment all too familiar, and euthanasia all too customary. They were confronted by the specters of endemic poverty, recurring famine, unfettered disease, and widespread chattel slavery—which the Christian West had only recently abolished. Cannibalism, ritual abuse, patricide, human sacrifice, sexual perversity, petty tyranny, paternalistic exploitation, live burials, exterminative clan warfare, and genocidal tribal vendettas all predominated.

Again and again, they had to affirm in the clearest possible way—in both word and deed—the singular message of light out of darkness, liberty out of tyranny, and life out of death. To cultures epidemic with terrible poverty, brutality, lawlessness, and disease, those faithful Christian witnesses interjected the novel Christian concepts of grace, charity, law, medicine, and the sanctity of life. They overturned despots, liberated the captives, and rescued the perishing. They established hospitals. They founded orphanages. They started rescue missions. They built almshouses. They opened soup kitchens. They incorporated charitable societies. They changed laws. They demonstrated love. They lived as if people really mattered.

Most of the missionaries knew that such a liberating message would likely be met with strident opposition. And it was. Anna Bowden's experience was by no means unique. Especially toward the end of the great missionary era—during the sunset of Victorianism—missionaries were often forced into conflicts with Europeans and North Americans who subscribed to the Enlightenment notions of Darwinism, Malthusianism, and eugenics.

As these ideas took a higher and higher profile at home, leaders in government and academia—and gradually even in the church—increasingly began to believe that the vast difference between Christian culture and pagan culture was actually not rooted in religion but in sociology and race. So Christian soldiers stationed in British colonies, for example, were often reprimanded for attending the baptisms of native converts because as representatives of the government, they were obligated to be "religiously neutral." Thus missionaries found it increasingly difficult to persuade the Western governments to abolish heathen customs and impose the rule of humanitarian law.

Alas, many even faced martyrdom. Such was the fate of Anna Bowden.

But death was not the end of Anna's impact. The "clash of absolutes" that she provoked highlighted for all the world to see the unbridgeable gulf between missionary ethics and colonial pragmatism. Her daring example sparked a revival within the missionary community in India, and her journals—published shortly after her martyrdom—made a stunning impact throughout England. Perhaps most important of all, her commitment stimulated and mobilized the church to call on the government to fundamentally alter the essence of the policy of noninterference—not just in India, but wherever missionaries went out around the globe—and to enforce a universal legal code rooted in the Christian notion of the sanctity of life.

Anna Bowden was a lady—an elect lady. And India in the nineteenth century was just the place for her.

Courage is a quality so necessary for maintaining virtue that it is always respected.

☙ *Anna Bowden (1852–1898)* ❧

Faith

*W*hat a man or woman does or does not believe is a matter of very little concern for most of us. We like to think that we can separate private from public concerns, character from performance, worldview from responsibility. Alas, such an innovative posture naturally carries a fearful implication. It really means that it does not matter what anyone of us believes so long as we do not take our beliefs seriously. But throughout history, wise men and women have understood that far from being a superfluous and private affair, our inmost faith is the utmost aspect of our outmost lives.

Man is what he believes.

Anton Chekhov (1860–1904)

There are no tricks in plain and simple faith.

William Shakespeare (c. 1564–1616)

A lie can only seize the mind of that man who has forgotten the Incarnation.

Andrew Nelson Lytle (1902–1995)

No abounding of material prosperity shall avail us if our spiritual senses atrophy. The foes of our own household will surely prevail against us unless there be in our people an inner life which finds its outer expression in a morality like unto that preached by the seers and prophets of God when the grandeur that was Greece and the glory that was Rome still lay in the future.

Theodore Roosevelt (1858–1919)

Faith, mighty faith,
The promise sees,
And looks to God alone;
Laughs at impossibilities,
And cries it shall be done.

Charles Wesley (1707–1788)

Faith is the force of life.

Leo Tolstoy (1828–1910)

We trust, not because a God exists, but because this God exists.

C. S. Lewis (1898–1963)

Strong Son of God, Immortal Love,
Whom we, that have not seen thy face,
By faith, and faith alone, embrace.

Alfred, Lord Tennyson (1809–1892)

Only the sheerest relativism insists that passing time renders unattainable one ideal while forcing upon us another.

Richard Weaver (1910–1963)

In one sense, Babylon is the acceptance of matter as the only meaning, the source of the mystery. That man could accept the shell for the total meaning, that his vanity could lead him a probing into can control matter and hence life, is the ultimate folly.

Andrew Nelson Lytle (1902–1995)

Faith is always at a disadvantage; it is a perpetually defeated thing which survives all conquerors.

G. K. Chesterton (1874–1936)

The great cleavage throughout the world lies between what is with, and what is against the faith.

Hilaire Belloc (1870–1953)

In the pioneer days of the West we found it an unfailing rule that after a community had existed for a certain length of time either a church was built or else the community began to go down hill. In those old communities in the Eastern States which have gone backward, it is noticeable that the retrogression has been both marked by and accentuated by a rapid decline in church membership and work; the two facts being so interrelated that each stands to the other partly as a cause and partly as an effect.

Theodore Roosevelt (1858–1919)

The hidden origin of all power, all suasion, and all purpose, is the assemblage of the covenant people: the church.

Samuel Johnson (1709–1784)

I never saw a moor,
I never saw the sea;
Yet know I how the heather looks,
And what a wave must be.

I never spoke with God,
Nor visited in heaven;
Yet certain am I of the spot
As if the chart were given.

Emily Dickinson (1830–1886)

God's in His heaven—
All's right with the world.

Robert Browning (1812–1889)

Many of our people, without knowing it, are Christian heathen, and demand as much missionary effort as the heathen of foreign lands.

Booker T. Washington (1856–1915)

By faith we know His existence, in glory we shall know His nature.
Blaise Pascal (1623–1662)

Call it faith, call it vitality, call it the will to live, call it the religion of tomorrow morning, call it the immortality of man, call it whatever you wish; it is the thing that explains why man survives all things and why there is no such thing as a pessimist.
G. K. Chesterton (1874–1936)

If I find in myself a desire which no experience in this world can satisfy, the most profitable explanation is that I was made for another world.
C. S. Lewis (1898–1963)

I try to avoid that species of intensely offensive spiritual pride which takes the form of sniggering conceit in being heterodox.
Theodore Roosevelt (1858–1919)

Sunset and evening star,
    And one clear call for me.
And may there be no moaning of the bar
    When I put out to sea.

But such a tide as moving seems asleep,
    Too full for sound and foam,
When that which drew from out the boundless deep
    Turns again home.

Twilight and evening bell,
    And after that the dark!
And may there be no sadness of farewell,
    When I embark.

For though from out our bourne of Time and Place
    The flood may bear me far,
I hope to see my Pilot face to face
    When I have crost the bar.

            Alfred, Lord Tennyson (1809–1892)

One does not discover new lands without consenting to lose sight of the shore.

            André Gide (1869–1951)

God has not called me to be successful; He has called me to be faithful.

Mother Teresa (1910–1997)

A churchless society is most assuredly a society on the downgrade.

Theodore Roosevelt (1858–1919)

Faith declares what the senses do not see, but not the contrary of what they see. It is above them, not contrary to them.

Blaise Pascal (1623–1662)

It is an equally awful truth that four and four makes eight, whether you reckon the thing out in eight onions or eight angels, eight bricks or eight bishops, eight minor poets or eight pigs. Similarly, if it be true that God made all things, that grave fact can be asserted by pointing at a star or by waving an umbrella.

G. K. Chesterton (1874–1936)

I can only say that I am nothing but a poor sinner, trusting in Christ alone for salvation.

Robert E. Lee (1807–1870)

Step out in faith.

Johann Sebastian Bach (1685–1750)

The Christian faith has not been tried and found wanting. It has been found difficult, and left untried.

G. K. Chesterton (1874–1936)

Faith begins to make one abandon the old way of judging. Averages and movements and the rest grow uncertain. The very nature of social force seems changed to us. And this is hard when a man has loved common views.

Hilaire Belloc (1870–1953)

Understanding is the reward of faith. Therefore seek not to understand that you may believe, but believe that you may understand.

Saint Augustine (354–430)

The motives to a life of faith are infinite.

Samuel Johnson (1709–1784)

Every thinking man, when he thinks, realizes that the teachings of the Bible are so interwoven and entwined with our whole civic and social life that it would be literally impossible for us to figure ourselves what that life would be if these standards were removed. We would lose almost all the standards by which we now judge both public and private morals; all the standards which we, with more or less resolution, strive to raise ourselves.

Theodore Roosevelt (1858–1919)

Basil of Caesarea and the Steadfastness of Belief

It was into a family of great wealth and distinction that Basil of Caesarea was born midway through the fourth century. Of all the great dynasties that mankind has seen emerge out of the sea of convention and commonality, perhaps none has left as permanent an impress on the course of history as that of the Cappadocian Valenzias. The Habsburgs, the Romanovs, and the Medicis were prodigious in their accomplishments. The Stuarts, the Bourbons, and the Mings were remarkable for their impact. The Warburgs, the Rothchilds, and the Carliles gave shape to one generation after another. But, the Valenzias outshone them all.

Basil's grandmother, Macri of Lyyra; his father Battia of Cappadocia; his mother, Emmelia of Athens; his sister, Macrina of Pontus; and his two younger brothers, Gregory of Nyssa and Peter of Sebastea, were all numbered among the early saints of the church. One of his other brothers, Paulus of Ry, became chief counsel to the emperor and still another, Stephen of Alexandria, became the imperial governor of Byzantium's largest colonial region. Three of his descendants eventually bore the imperial scepter and two others ascended to the ecumenical throne. For more than a thousand years some member of this remarkable family held a high position in Constantinople's corridors of power and influence.

But as great as his family was, Basil was himself, greater still.

Renowned for his encyclopedic learning, he studied in all the great schools of his day—in Caesarea, Constantinople, Athens, and Rome. For a short time he practiced law with an eye toward a public career, but he determined to heed a call into the ministry instead. He helped to establish a Christian community in Annesi where he distinguished himself as a man of extraordinary charity and brilliance. It was not long before his reputation reached the farthest edges of the empire. He was a quick-witted adversary to the heretical Arians; he was a valiant defender of orthodoxy; he had a productive theological pen; and he was a man who combined a deep and sincere piety with a tough and realistic practicality. In short order, he was called to the very prominent parish ministry of Caesarea.

Because he believed that faith meant that every aspect of life ought to be informed by the Gospel, he undertook the task of total integration—it was not merely the realm of the spirit, but every arena, every detail, every endeavor that was to be transformed. Diligent to perform his pastoral duties, Basil soon found himself overwhelmed with busyness. He led eighteen services every week—except just before Christmas and Easter when there were more—in addition to his work of catechizing the young, visiting the sick, and encouraging the distressed. He also kept up a heavy correspondence and continued his theological output. Despite all this, he was able to involve himself in the issues and concerns of the day. He was deeply moved by the plight of the poor and spent the rest of his life seeking practical ways to alleviate their suffering and to facilitate their recovery. He instituted the practice of almsgiving in Caesarea, utilizing the resources of the church to create new opportunities for the needy and to transform their poverty into productivity. Because health care is an important part of that process, and because the poor were generally denied access to anything but the crassest form of folk medicine, Basil opened the very first nonambulatory hospital.

It was his involvement with the poor and his work in the hospital that ultimately led Basil into a confrontation with still another series of societal woes: infanticide, exposure, and abandonment. Despite the fact that Christianity had obtained official status some forty years earlier, the Cappadocian region was not yet thoroughly evangelized and a number of pagan practices persisted—including callous and heedless child-killing.

Basil was horrified.

He discovered an underground guild of occultists, or *sagae*, that were doing a booming trade in Caesarea and the surrounding environs. They provided herbal potions, pessaries, and even surgical remedies for women who wished to avoid childbearing. The bodies of the children were then harvested and sold to cosmetolgists in Egypt—who used the collagen for the manufacture of various beauty creams.

When Basil approached several city officials about the horrors that the *sagae* were perpetrating on the women and children of the community, he was shocked to discover that the awful trade was perfectly legal—and always had been.

Immediately he sprang into action. He preached a series of sermons on the sanctity of human life; he mobilized the members of his church to help care for families and women who were facing crisis pregnancies; he began to exercise the full weight of his family influence as well as his own considerable powers of persuasion to change the laws; he began an education program throughout the entire city so that people could fully understand the issues; he took imprecatory ecclesiastical action against the *sagae*, declaring them to be anathema; and he even staged public protests against the Egyptian traders who helped to support the grisly trade with their mercantile ingenuity.

But that was by no means the end of the matter. Precedents legitimately tenured and deeply rooted would not be easily dispatched. According to the centuries' old tradition of paterfamilias, the birth of a Roman was not a biological fact. Infants were received into the world only as the family willed. A Roman did not have a child; he took a child. Immediately after birthing, if the family decided not to raise the child—literally lifting him above the earth—he was simply abandoned. There were special high places or walls, outside most Roman cities where the newborn was taken and exposed to die.

Basil had heard of exposure, but he was amazed to discover that it too was still perfectly legal—and was, at least to some limited degree, still practiced. So he broadened his attentions, not only opposing the *sagae*, but also lobbying to have paterfamilias abrogated, the exposure walls decimated, and the high places brought down.

So passionate was Basil in his concern for life that apparently, late one evening after vespers, he and several deacons from the church actually went outside the city to dismantle the old Caesarean infanticide shrine with their bare hands. He knew that such direct action could very well jeopardize his standing, but he was driven by an irrepressible spiritual imperative.

Hearing of Basil's solitary crusade, the Emperor Valentinian took the first step toward the full criminalization of infanticide in 374.

For the first time in human history, abortion, infanticide, exposure, and abandonment were made illegitimate. The *sagae* were driven underground and eventually out of business altogether. The tradition of paterfamilias was all but overturned. The exposure walls were destroyed. And the high places were brought low.

When Basil died just four years later at the age of fifty, he had not only made his mark on the church, he had altered the course of human history—

and he had laid the groundwork for the flowering of one of the greatest family dynasties mankind has ever known.

His life was a testimony to the comprehensiveness of faith—the total integration of truth and life. There was no possibility of separation for him—otherwise, faith might become little more than a lost cause. Instead, faith was to be the defining feature of his all in all.

If faith produce no works, I see
That faith is not a living tree.
Thus faith and works together grow,
No separate life they e'er can know:
They're soul and body, hand and heart;
What God hath joined, let no man part.

&ſ *Basil of Caesarea (c. 330–379)* ſə

Wisdom

*W*e admire knowledge. We covet understanding. But we tend to be
more than a little suspicious of wisdom. It is a notion that seems to
carry with it the taint of dusty ideals and musty aspirations. It has
the appearance of advanced age—and all the out-of-fashion traits of
reticence, hesitation, caution, recalcitrance, and anachronism that go
with decrepitude. Even so, throughout ages past, men and nations
have cherished wisdom as more than wishful thinking or hopeful
yearning. They have acknowledged its vital role in stable societies
and healthy cultures.

To know that which before us lies in daily life is the prime wisdom.
John Milton (1608–1674)

This is a practice as full of labor as a wise man's art, for folly that he wisely shows is fit,
but wise men, folly—fall'n, quite taint their wit.
William Shakespeare (c. 1564–1616)

Only for a little of the first fruits of wisdom—only a few fragments of the boundless heights, breadths, and depths of truth—does the world yearn for from our table of grace.
Martin Luther (1483–1546)

They say you may praise a fool till you make him useful: I don't know much about that, but I do know that if I get a bad knife I generally cut my finger, and a blunt axe is far more trouble than profit. A handsaw is a good thing, but not to shave with.
Charles H. Spurgeon (1834–1892)

There are, indeed, many truths which time necessarily and certainly teaches, and which might, by those who have learned them from experience, be communicated to their successors at a cheaper rate: but dictates, though liberally enough bestowed, are generally without effect, the teacher gains few proselytes by instruction which his own behaviour contradicts; and young men miss the benefit of counsel, because they are not very ready to believe that those who fall below them in practice, can much excel them in theory. Thus the progress of knowledge is retarded, the world is kept long in the same state, and every new race is to gain the prudence of their predecessors by committing and redressing the same miscarriages.

Samuel Johnson (1709–1784)

Education is not the filling of a pail but the lighting of a fire. Of such is wisdom.

William Butler Yeats (1865–1939)

Forewarned, forearmed; to be prepared is half the victory. Wisdom comes of such a recognition.

Miguel de Cervantes (1547–1616)

The next best thing to being wise onself is to live in a circle of those who are.

C. S. Lewis (1898–1963)

Understanding is knowing what to do; wisdom is knowing what to do next; virtue is actually doing it.

Tristan Gylberd (1954–)

A wise old owl sat on an oak;
The more he saw the less he spoke;
The less he spoke the more he heard;
Why aren't we like that wise old bird?

Edward Richards (1842–1911)

I would have everybody able to read, and write, and cipher; indeed I don't think a man can know too much; but mark you, the knowing of these things is not education; and there are millions of your reading and writing people who are as ignorant as neighbor Norton's calf, that did not know its own mother.

Charles H. Spurgeon (1834–1892)

What you do when you don't have to, determines what you will be when you can no longer help it.

Rudyard Kipling (1865–1936)

Wisdom is found only in truth.

Johann von Goethe (1749–1832)

To be genuinely wise, one must make haste slowly.

Benjamin Franklin (1706–1790)

Instruct a wise man and he will be wiser still; teach a righteous man and he will add to his learning.

King Solomon (c. 1000 B.C.)

The art of being wise is the art of knowing what to overlook.

William James (1842–1910)

To be wise, one must take time to deliberate. But when the time for action has arrived, one must stop deliberating and boldly act.

Napoleon Bonaparte (1769–1821)

Go for to life, oh child of earth,
Still mindful of thy heavenly birth;
Thou art not here for ease or sin,
But manhood's noble crown to win.

Though passion's fires are in thy soul,
Thy spirit can their flames control;
Though tempters strong beset thy way,
Thy spirit is more strong than they.

Go on from innocence of youth;
To manly pureness, manly truth;
God's angels still are near to save,
And God himself doth help the brave.

Then forth to life, oh child of earth,
Be worthy of thy heavenly birth,
For noble service thou art here;
Thy brothers help, thy God revere.

Henry Wadsworth Longfellow (1807–1882)

Learn from the mistakes of others—you don't have nearly enough time to make them all yourself.

Tristan Gylberd (1954–)

A wise man will make more opportunities than he finds.

Francis Bacon (1561–1626)

Nothing is more common than for men to make partial and absurd distinctions between vices of equal enormity, and to observe some of the divine commands with great scrupulousness, while they violate others, equally important, without any concern, or the least apparent consciousness of guilt. Alas, it is only wisdom which perceives this tragedy.

Samuel Johnson (1709–1784)

The heart of a fool is in his mouth, but the mouth of a wise man is in his heart.

Benjamin Franklin (1706–1790)

When I was a boy of 14, my father was so ignorant I could hardly stand to have the old man around. But when I got to be 21, I was astonished at how much the old man had learned in seven years.

Mark Twain (1835–1910)

That which seems to be the height of absurdity in one generation often becomes the height of wisdom in the next.

John Stuart Mill (1806–1873)

The wise does at once what the fool does at last.

Baltasar Gracián (1601–1658)

A man is wise as long as he searches for wisdom; he becomes a fool the moment he thinks he has found it.

Tristan Gylberd (1954–)

O world, thou choosest not the better part!
It is not wisdom to be only wise,
And on the inward vision close the eyes,
But it is wisdom to believe the heart.
Columbus found a world, and had no chart,
Save one that faith deciphered in the skies;
To trust the soul's invincible surmise
Was all his science and his only art.

George Santayana (1863–1952)

A prudent question is one-half of wisdom.
Francis Bacon (1561–1626)

Knowledge is proud that he has learned so much;
Wisdom is humble that he knows no more.
William Cowper (1731–1800)

Never be ashamed to own you have been in the wrong; 'tis but saying you are wiser today than yesterday.
Jonathan Swift (1667–1745)

A wise man will not leave the right to the mercy of chance, nor wish it to prevail through the power of the majority. There is but little virtue in the action of masses of men.
Henry David Thoreau (1817–1862)

Nine-tenths of wisdom is being wise in time.
Theodore Roosevelt (1858–1919)

Knowledge comes, but wisdom lingers.
Alfred, Lord Tennyson (1809–1892)

Wisdom is oft times nearer when we stoop than when we soar.
William Wordsworth (1770–1850)

To establish the fact of decadence is the most pressing duty of wisdom in our time.
Richard Weaver (1910–1963)

The fear of the Lord is the beginning of wisdom and knowledge of the Holy One is understanding.
King Solomon (c. 1000 B.C.)

Jonathan Edwards and the Struggle for Substance

Unlike his friend George Whitefield, Jonathan Edwards was not a particularly enthralling master of pulpit theatrics or hermaneutical technique. Instead, he won his reputation as a thinker. He was highly regarded as a "precise dogmatician." He was widely admired as a "careful systemizer." And he was deeply appreciated as a "cogent preceptor."

As a philosopher, his greatness was unmatched. Thomas Chalmers said that he was "undoubtedly the greatest of all the theologians." Benjamin Franklin said that he "had a rational mind unmatched for generations untold." Daniel Webster said that his books were among the "greatest achievements of the human intellect." James Hollister said he was "the most gifted man of the eighteenth century, perhaps the most profound thinker in the world." Robert Hall said that "he was the greatest of the sons of men." Moses Tyler said he was "the most original and acute thinker yet produced in America." And Georges Lyon said he was "superior to Locke, Newton, Descartes, and a couple of Pascals combined."

But as a preacher, he apparently left a little something to be desired. In fact, he read his densely theological and tautly philosophical sermons from painstakingly researched longhand manuscripts—often in a flat, monotonous voice. Only rarely did he deign to make eye contact with his congregation. Though not unpleasant in demeanor, he hardly cut a dashing or charismatic figure.

A member of his church described these deficiencies sympathetically. "His appearance in the pulpit was with a good grace, and his delivery easy, natural, but very solemn. He had not a strong voice but appeared with such gravity, and spake with such distinctness and precision—his words so full of ideas and set in such a plain and striking light—that few speakers have been so able to demand the attention of an audience as he. His words often discovered a great degree of inward fervor, without much noise or external emotion, and fell with great weight on the minds of his hearers. He made but little motion of his head or hands in the pulpit, but spake as to discover the motion of his own heart, which tended in the most natural and effectual manner to move and affect others."

But another said: "I can little explain how the assembly remains awake during his discourses—which are over-long, boorish, and often incomprehensible to the simple man. Though there is evidence of some great passion in thought, yet to the eye and ear, little or none."

Nevertheless, on July 8, 1741, Edwards traveled a few miles from his home into western Connecticut and read to a small congregation assembled there "the most famous sermon ever delivered in the history of America."

Entitled "Sinners in the Hands of An Angry God," the sermon was an exposition of the text, "Their foot shall slide in due time" (Deuteronomy 32:35). Its subject was the imminence of judgment and the horrors of perdition. It was about what we today derisively call "hell-fire and damnation."

Later described by literary and historical critics as a "rhetorical masterpiece," the sermon was astonishingly gripping and terrifyingly vivid: "Yea, God is a great deal more angry with great numbers that are now on the earth; yea doubtless, with many that are now in this congregation, who it may be are at ease, than He is with many of those who are now in the flames of Hell. The wrath of God burns against them, their damnation does not slumber; the pit is prepared, the fire is made ready; the furnace is now hot ready to receive them; the flames do now rage and glow; the glittering sword is now whet and held over them. Unconverted men walk over the pit of Hell on a rotten covering, and there are innumerable places in this covering so weak that they will not bear their own weight, and these places are not seen."

The sermon caused an immediate sensation in the town of Enfield where it was preached. According to historian John Currid, even before the sermon was finished, "people were moaning, groaning and crying out" such things as "What shall I do to be saved?" In fact, there was such a "breathing of distress and weeping" that Edwards had to quiet and calm the people several times so he could conclude. The fervor of the Great Awakening that had thus far bypassed Enfield now swept through the little town with a white-hot intensity. Suddenly the people were "bowed down with an awful conviction of their sin and danger." And a "great outpouring of the Holy Spirit" came with "amazing and astonishing power" evidenced by the fact that "several souls were wrought upon" in that place of "former antipathy."

In short order the sermon was printed and widely distributed through-out the American colonies. It not only won for Edwards even greater renown than he already enjoyed, but it provoked a further awakening among its distant readers. Since then it has been reprinted hundreds of times—perhaps thousands. To this day it is not only a standard text for the study of great preaching, it has passed into the realm of classic literature—and thus is the most anthologized sermon in the English language.

Though obviously anointed with divine favor, "Sinners in the Hands of an Angry God"—like so much of the rest of his vast body of work—was not without controversy. Many said that Edwards illegitimately played upon people's emotions. Others said that he shamelessly exploited the popular fears and phobias of the day. Still others said that he appealed to the innate intolerance, bigotry, and mob instincts of unsuspecting simple-minded people.

For the record, Edwards claimed that all of his sermons—and there were many on the subject of Hell, some even more vivid than the one he preached in Enfield—were modeled on the admonition of the Apostle Paul, "Knowing therefore the terror of the Lord, we persuade men" (2 Corinthians 5:11). He told his own parish, "I don't desire to go about to terrify you needlessly or represent your case worse than it is, but I do verily think that there are a number of people belonging to this congregation in imminent danger of being damned to all eternity."

It was that kind of pastoral concern and evangelistic passion that enabled Edwards to wisely lend leadership and direction to the Great Awakening—perhaps the most sweeping revival in modern history. It enabled him to become the "acknowledged dean" of American Evangelicalism. And it thrust him into the international limelight alongside Whitefield and Wesley as a spokesman for Christian unity and cooperation.

Even so, the controversy stirred by his unbending commitment to an unadulterated substantiveness never entirely went away. After nearly a quarter century of service to his Northampton congregation, a small disgruntled faction—advocates of what historian Perry Miller called a kind of "early pluralism" who desired less stringent moral standards for church membership than Edwards would allow—secured his ouster. They were apparently offended by his insistence that the message of justice—temporal and eternal—was inseparable from the message of faith. He was exiled to the frontier where he lived out his days as a missionary to the Indians.

But he had no regrets. He knew that the substantiveness of the faith was not a matter to be trifled with. He knew that both the imminence and the finality of eternal judgment mitigated against lowering the standards, diluting the ethics, or compromising the integrity of his proclamations. He knew that Hell was the best argument against muddled and mitigated morals. His position was simple: "The Good News is that the bad news is bad—and yet hope remains." Knowing this, Jonathan Edwards threw caution to the wind and pled for his congregation to hear and heed a message of substantive wisdom: "You hang by a slender thread, with the flames of divine wrath flashing about it, and ready every moment to singe it and burn it asunder. God hath had it on His heart to show angels and men, both how excellent His love is, and also how terrible His wrath is."

He was unwilling—regardless of the cost—to dumb down his message, to make it more user-friendly, to reduce it to the lowest common denominator. He was convinced that to do so would be a betrayal of wisdom. As G. K. Chesterton later remarked, "If the world grows too worldly, it can be rebuked by the church; but if the church grows too worldly, it cannot be adequately rebuked for worldliness by the world." So Edwards stuck by his guns.

Cost him, it did. His struggle for substantiveness appeared to be a lost cause toward the end of his life. But in the end his weighty refusal to compromise ensured his reputation. Today no one reads the critics of Jonathan Edwards; no one takes seriously their arguments; no one even considers their concerns. As Shakespeare asserted, "Wisdom will always out in the end."

Resolved: Never to do anything which I should be afraid to do if it were the last hour of my life.

Jonathan Edwards (1703–1758)

Truthfulness

*W*e might admire the truth, but rarely do we really want to hear it. We prefer a sugar-coated version of human events. We are unabashedly partial to perspectives slanted in our favor. But unhampered and unfettered truth is the only ground upon which honest, open, and free relationships may be built—whether in families and communities or among societies and nations. Wisdom, as it has been expressed through all the ages, has always welcomed the truth, the whole truth, and nothing but the truth.

Tis strange—but true; for truth is always strange;
Stranger than fiction.
Lord Byron (1788–1824)

Truth is such a rare thing, it is delightful to tell it.
Emily Dickinson (1830–1886)

Nonsense is nonsense whether it rhymes or not, just as bad half-pennies are good for nothing whether they jingle or lie quiet.
Charles H. Spurgeon (1834–1892)

The man who knows the truth and has the opportunity to tell it, but who nonetheless refuses to, is among the most shameful of all creatures. God forbid that we should ever become so lax as that.
Theodore Roosevelt (1858–1919)

The mercy of truth is to be truth.
Laura Riding (1901–1991)

Let liars fear, let cowards shrink,
Let traitors turn away;
Whatever we have dared to think,
That we dare to say.

ᛜ *James Russell Lowell (1819–1891)* ᛜ

Truth may be stretched but cannot be broken, and always gets above false-hood, as oil does above water.

ᛜ *Miguel de Cervantes (1547–1616)* ᛜ

Error lives but a day. Truth is eternal.

ᛜ *James Longstreet (1821–1904)* ᛜ

Not to scatter bread and gold,
Goods and rainment bought and sold;
But to hold fast his simple sense
And speek the speech of innocence:
And with hand and body and blood,
To make his bosom counsel good.
He that feeds men serveth few;
He serves all who dares to be true.

ᛜ *Ralph Waldo Emerson (1808–1882)* ᛜ

A man always has two reasons for doing anything: a good reason and the real reason. Let us be like the man of the frontier and always reveal with utmost honesty our real reasons for all that we do.

J. P. Morgan (1837–1913)

He that is warm for truth, and fearless in its defense, performs one of the duties of a good man; he strengthens his own conviction, and guards others from delusion; but steadiness of belief, and boldness of profession, are yet only part of the form of godliness.

Samuel Johnson (1709–1784)

An honest man's the noblest work of God.

Alexander Pope (1688–1744)

I hope I shall always possess firmness and virtue enough to maintain what I consider the most enviable of all titles, the character of an honest man.

George Washington (1732–1799)

· *Truthfulness* ·

A little integrity is better than any career.
Ralph Waldo Emerson (1803–1882)

No legacy is so rich as honesty.
William Shakespeare (c. 1564–1616)

Every honest man will suppose honest acts to flow from honest principles.
Thomas Jefferson (1743–1826)

How happy is he born or taught
That serveth not another's will;
Whose armor is his honest thought
And simple truth his utmost skill.
Henry Wotton (1568–1639)

The enemies of the truth are always awfully nice.
Christopher Morely (1890–1957)

Since the time of Bacon the world has been running away from, rather than toward, first principles, so that, on the verbal level, we see fact substituted for truth.
Richard Weaver (1910–1963)

There is no well-defined boundary line between honesty and dishonesty. The frontiers of one blend with the outside limits of the other, and he who attempts to tread this dangerous ground may be sometimes in the one domain and sometimes in the other.
O. Henry (1862–1910)

The greatest homage we can pay to truth is to use it.
Ralph Waldo Emerson (1803–1882)

Truth: that long, clean, clear, simple, undeniable, unchallengable, straight, and shining line, on one side of which is black and on the other of which is white.

William Faulkner (1897–1962)

You cannot drive straight on a twisting lane.

John Buchan (1875–1940)

A lie stands on one leg, truth on two.

Benjamin Franklin (1706–1790)

Opinion is a flitting thing
But truth outlasts the sun;
If we cannot own them both,
Possess the oldest one.

Emily Dickinson (1830–1886)

The brilliant passes, like the dew at morn;
The true endures, for ages yet unborn.

Johann von Goethe (1749–1832)

If you tell the truth you don't have to remember anything.

Mark Twain (1835–1910)

Truth, crushed to earth, shall rise again.
The eternal years of God are hers.

William Cullen Bryant (1794–1878)

Truth is the trial of itself,
And needs no other touch;
And purer than the purest gold,
Refine it ne'er so much.

Ben Jonson (1572–1637)

Such is the irresistible nature of truth that all it asks, and all it wants, is the liberty of appearing.

Thomas Paine (1737–1809)

I had rather starve and rot and keep the privilege of speaking the truth than of holding all the offices that capital has to give, from the presidency downward.

Henry Adams (1838–1918)

Commend me to sterling honesty, though clad in rags.

Sir Walter Scott (1771–1832)

Genuine simplicity of heart is a healing and cementing principle.

Edmund Burke (1729–1797)

My worth to God in public is what I am in private.
Oswald Chambers (1874–1917)

Aye, sir; to be honest, as this world goes, is to be one man picked out of ten thousand.
William Shakespeare (c. 1564–1616)

The honest man takes pains, and then enjoys pleasures; the knave takes pleasure, and then suffers pains.
Benjamin Franklin (1706–1790)

Make yourself an honest man, and then you will be sure there is one rascal less in the world.
Thomas Carlyle (1795–1881)

Some books are lies frae end to end
And some great lies were never pen'd:
Ev'n ministers, they hae been ken'd,
In holy rapture,
A rousin whid at times to vend
An' nail't wi' Scripture.

But this that I am gaun to tell,
Which lately on a night befell,
Is just as true's the deil's in hell
Or Dublin city:
That e'er he nearer comes oursel
'S a muckle pity.

ᘍ *Robert Burns (1759–1796)* ᘔ

Clear and round dealing is the honor of a man's nature, and that mixture of falsehood is like alloy in coin of gold and silver, which makes the metal work the better, but debases it.

ᘍ *Francis Bacon (1561–1626)* ᘔ

Truth is that golden chain
It links together the terrestrial,
With that greater plane,
Which is but glorious celestial.

Truth sets the seal of heaven
On all the things of this sphere,
And infuses with the leaven
That maketh life so dear.

Simon Fraser (1776–1862)

He that acknowledges the obligations of morality, and pleases his vanity
with enforcing them to others, concludes himself zealous in the cause of
virtue, though he has no longer any regard to her precepts, than they con-
form to his own desires; and counts himself among her warmest lovers,
because he praises her beauty, though every rival steals away his heart.

Samuel Johnson (1709–1784)

Vincent de Paul and the Spirit of the Age

The remarkable explosion of wealth, knowledge, and technology that occurred during the Renaissance and the Enlightenment completely reshaped human society. No institution was left untouched.

Families were transformed from mere digits within the larger baronial or communal clan into nuclear societies in and of themselves. Local communities were shaken from their sleepy timidity and thrust into the hustle bustle of mercantilism and urbanization. The church was rocked by the convulsions of the Reformation, the Counter Reformation, Anabaptism, deism, and neopaganism. Kingdoms, fiefs, baronies, and principalities began to take the torturous path toward becoming modern nation states.

Such revolutionary changes are not without cost. Ultimately, the cost to Western civilization was devastating. Immorality and corruption ran rampant. Disparity between rich and poor became endemic. Ruthless and petty wars multiplied beyond number. Even the old horrors of abortion, infanticide, abandonment, and exposure began to recur in the urban and industrialized centers.

Vincent De Paul was born for such a time as this—to tackle such problems as these.

Raised the son of a peasant farmer in Gascony, he surrendered to the ministry at the age of twenty. Spurred on by a passionate concern for the poor and neglected, he quickly developed a thriving outreach to the decayed gentry, deprived peasantry, galleyslaves, unwanted children, and convicts of France. Over the ensuing years, he mobilized hundreds of

Christians for charitable work and established innumerable institutions—hospitals, shelters, foundling centers, orphanages, and almshouses throughout all of Europe.

Despite its many advances in art, music, medicine, science, and technology, the Renaissance and Enlightenment were essentially nostalgic revivals of ancient pagan ideals and values. The dominating ideas of the times were classical humanism, pregnable naturalism, and antinomian individualism—or in other words: godlessness, materialism, and hedonism. Taking their cues primarily from ancient Greece and Rome, the leaders of the epoch were not so much interested in the Christian notion of progress as they were in the heathen ideal of innocence. Reacting to the artificialities and contrivances of the medieval period, they dispatched the Christian consensus it had wrought with enervating aplomb. In short, they threw the baby out with the bath.

Throughout history men have reacted instead of acted in times of crisis. They have sought to ameliorate an ill on the right hand by turning immediately and entirely to the left. They have tried to solve a problem in the citadels of the present by desecrating the foundations of the past. Driven by extremism, they have failed to see the moderating application of adjustments and alternatives.

We fall into that same trap today. Instead of attempting to reform, refurbish, or renovate, we tend to want to rip asunder the roots of the ages and start over from scratch. The result of such ludicrous impudence is invariably disastrous. When faced with economic inequity and injustice, our first reaction is to bureaucratically centralize the means of production and distribution—instead of actually creating new opportunities and incentives for the poor. When faced with the problem of hunger in the Third World, our inclination is to sterilize mothers, denude traditional authority, and collectivize property—instead of actually promoting development projects that can help transform poverty into productivity.

When faced with the recalcitrance of feudal life, the immediate reaction of the people of the Renaissance and Enlightenment was to reject out of hand the very foundations of their Christian heritage—instead of actually building on that heritage for the future. Nothing was sacred any longer. Everything—every thought, word, and deed, every hope, dream, and aspiration, every tradition, institution, and relationship—was redefined.

No society can long stand without some ruling set of principles, some overriding values, or some ethical standard. Thus, when the men and women of the sixteenth through the eighteenth centuries threw off Christian mores, they necessarily went casting about for a suitable alternative. And so, Greek and Roman thought was exhumed from the ancient sarcophagus of paganism. Aristotle, Plato, and Pythagoras were dusted off, dressed up, and rehabilitated as the newly tenured voices of wisdom. Cicero, Seneca, and Herodotus were raised from the philosophical crypt and made to march to the tune of a new era.

Every forum, every arena, and every aspect of life began to reflect this newfound fascination with the pre-Christian past. Art, architecture, music, drama, literature, and every other form of popular culture began to portray the themes of classical humanism, pregnable naturalism, and antinomian individualism.

Because prosperity during that time was widespread and because personal peace and affluence had become the principal virtues of polite society, very few wanted to hear of social injustice. People did not want to hear about problems. It was offensive to them to hear that all was not well in their world. Very simply, the unvarnished truth put them off—much as it does in our own day.

But Vincent believed that it was his duty to tell the truth at all times and in every situation—however unpopular that truth might be. Thus it seemed that the great effect of his preaching was to make everybody feel condemned, and nobody likes that. But then, he was in good company—Jesus Himself had that same propensity.

On almost every page of the New Testament, we find Jesus offending someone. When He wasn't confronting the Scribes and the Pharisees, He was rebuking the promiscuous and the perverse. When He wasn't alienating the Sadducees and the Herodians, He was reproving the tax collectors and the prostitutes. He even had a knack for estranging His own disciples with His "hard sayings" and "dark parables."

Jesus "meek and mild" was rarely meek or mild when it came to sin. He pulled no punches. Indeed, at various times, and when the situation demanded, Jesus publicly denounced sinners as snakes, dogs, foxes, hypocrites, fouled tombs, and dirty dishes. He actually referred to one of His chief disciples as Satan. So that His hearers would not miss the point, He sometimes referred to the objects of his most intense ridicule both by name and by position, and often face to face.

He was an equal opportunity offender. He told the truth.

Vincent felt that he could do no less. He realized, of course, that such a message was never intended to be popular; it was intended to be true. He knew that there was no justice in a killing kindness; it may be attained only in the brutal apprehension of man's dire need of Christ. He was convinced that everyone desperately needed Good News, not nice news.

And that was simply not a popular notion. Not then. Not now. Not ever.

The societal experts then—as well they might today—told Vincent that controversial or confrontational preaching does more to drive people away than to draw them in. They told him that sermons ought to appeal to the lowest common denominator, that services ought to be simple and accessible, and that programs ought to be consumer-oriented and user-friendly— otherwise he might offend rather than attract. They told him that substantive theology would at best confuse the average churchgoer, and at worst, alienate him.

And they were probably right—as the ministry of Jesus so amply demonstrated. His insistence that the demands of justice ultimately had to be satisfied in unadulterated truth was an affront to virtually everyone who heard Him.

It still is.

Despite the fact that the free spirit of the Renaissance and the early Enlightenment had swept across the culture like a prairie fire, Vincent's efforts to tell the truth in both word and deed struck a responsive note among a faithful remnant. They rejected the siren's song of the day and embraced the values and virtues of truth. They developed a comprehensive plan of service to the needy and a concerted program of opposition to patterns of injustice.

Vincent made it clear to his fellow laborers that such activity is not an option for the believer—it is mandatory. He said, "When'ere God's people gather, there is life in the midst of them—yea, Christ's gift to us as a people is life, and that more abundantly. To protect the least of these, our brethren, with everything that God has placed at our disposal is not merely facultative, it is exigent. In addition though, it is among the greatest and most satisfying of our sundry stewardships. Of such is truth."

By the time he died in 1660, the charitable relief movement he had sparked was alive and well—alert to the threat against the innocents that inevitably comes when men turn their hearts away from Christian truth and toward the delusions of this world. To this day all around the globe, members of the Society of Vincent de Paul continue the momentum that he began by modeling a life of obedience to the truth.

We who are named of the truth have a mandate to not merely love in word and tongue but in action and truth. Thus, our unanimity on the matter must not merely be rhetorical. It must be translated into action.

Vincent de Paul (1581–1660)

Manhood

The feminization of modern Western culture has meant a denigration of virtually every aspect of masculinity. Manly pursuits, inclinations, and aspirations are mockingly derided as veritably Neanderthal by everyone from political prognosticators to social scientists and everything from television sitcoms to pop music videos. The boldness, decisiveness, and assertiveness of male leadership has become woefully politically incorrect. It is a lost cause. But through the ages, the standards of courageous, dynamic, and substantive manliness has always been highly esteemed by astute observers of the human condition.

The wicked flee when no one pursues, but the righteous are bold as a lion.

◆꜠ *King Solomon (c. 1000 B.C.)* ꜠◆

The emasculation of society by the smothering effects of modern uniformity has precipitated a severely over-managed, sadly under-led, and passionately un-principled culture from top to bottom. The great cry for the renewal of our civilization is for men to arise and be men.

◆꜠ *Tristan Gylberd (1954–)* ꜠◆

Beyond the poet's sweet dream lives
The eternal epic of the man.

◆꜠ *John Greenleaf Whittier (1807–1892)* ꜠◆

Weasel words from mollycoddles will never do when the day demands prophetic clarity from greathearts. Manly men must emerge for this hour of trial.

◆꜠ *Theodore Roosevelt (1858–1919)* ꜠◆

Finally, my brethren, be strong in the Lord and in the power of His might. Put on the whole armor of God, that you may be able to stand against the wiles of the devil. For we do not wrestle against flesh and blood, but against principalities, against powers, against the rulers of the darkness of this age, against spiritual hosts of wickedness in the heavenly places. Therefore take up the whole armor of God, that you may be able to withstand in the evil day, and having done all, to stand. Stand therefore, having girded your waist with truth, having put on the breastplate of righteousness, and having shod your feet with the preparation of the gospel of peace; above all, taking the shield of faith with which you will be able to quench all the fiery darts of the wicked one. And take the helmet of salvation, and the sword of the Spirit, which is the word of God.

Paul of Tarsus (c. 10–65)

Well, if we are to die, let us die like men.

Patrick Cleburne (1831–1864)

Boldness is prudence. Courage is manliness.

James Longstreet (1821–1904)

Awake, awake, put on strength, Awake as in the ancient days, in the generations of old.

Isaiah of Jerusalem (c. 750 B.C.)

We have already lost nearly all but honor by the last war, and I must say, that in order to be men, we must protect our honor at all hazards and thus, preserve our homes and families and whatever else may be left.

Nathan Bedford Forrest (1821–1877)

Far better it is to dare mighty things, to win glorious triumphs, even though checkered by failure, than to take rank with those poor spirits who neither enjoy much nor suffer much because they live in the gray twilight that knows neither victory nor defeat.

Theodore Roosevelt (1858–1919)

Be men.

Paul of Tarsus (c. 10–65)

A nation needs manly heroes. It needs examples of valor so that it will know just how it ought to behave.

Theodore Roosevelt (1858–1919)

A bold Christian is the highest style of a man.

Thomas Young (1722–1799)

For God has not given us a spirit of fear, but of power and of love and of a sound mind.

Paul of Tarsus (c. 10–65)

He has done the work of a true man,
Crown him, honor him, love him.
Weep over him, tears of woman,
Stoop manliest brows over him.

No duty could overtask him,
No need his will outrun;
Or ever our lips could ask him,
His hand the work had done.

John Greenleaf Whittier (1807–1892)

See the same man in vigor, in the gout;
Alone, in company, in place, or out;
Early at business, and at hazard late;
Mad at a fox chase, wise at debate;
Grogged at a borough, civil at a ball;
Friendly at Hackney, faithless at Whitehall.

Alexander Pope (1688–1744)

Is there, for honest poverty,
That hings his head, an' a' that?
The coward slave, we pass him by,
We dare be poor for a' that!
For a' that, an' a' that,
Our toils obscure, an' a' that;
The rank is but the guinea's stamp;
The man's the gowd for a' that.

What tho' on hamely fare we dine,
Wear hodden gray, an' a' that;
Gie fools their silks, and knaves their wine,
A man's a man for a' that,
For a' that, an' a' that,
Their tinsel show, an' a' that;
The honest man, tho' e'er sae poor,
Is king o' men for a' that.

Ye see yon birkie, ca'd a lord,
Wha struts, an' stares, an' a' that;
Tho' hundreds worship at his word,
He's but a coof for a' that:

For a' that, an' a' that,
His riband, star, an' a' that,
The man o' independent mind,
He looks and laughs at a' that.

A prince can mak a belted knight,
A marquis, duke, an' a' that;
But an honest man's aboon his might,
Guid faith he mauna fa' that!
For a' that, an' a' that,
Their dignities, an' a' that,
The pith o' sense, an' pride o' worth,
Are higher rank than a' that.

Then let us pray that come it may,
As come it will for a' that,
That sense and worth, o'er a' the earth,
May bear the gree, an' a' that.
For a' that, an' a' that,
It's coming yet, for a' that,
That man to man, the world o'er,
Shall brothers be for a' that.

Robert Burns (1759–1796)

JOHN BUCHAN AND THE IDEAL OF MANLINESS

Throughout his life he sought out adventure. He was brash in his leadership. He was gentlemanly in his demeanor. He was voracious in his appetites. He was passionate in his enthusiasms. In every way imaginable, John Buchan was a man's man.

He loved the mystery, the beauty, and the majesty of creation. Almost every aspect of his life—from the way he raised his children to the way he conducted his politics, from the way he spent his leisure time to the way he pursued his intellectual interests, from the way he related to other men to the way he invested his resources—revolved around his manly love for the natural world.

He spent almost every minute he could outdoors. His enthusiastic involvement in hiking through the woods, riding horseback across the fields, hunting in the wilderness, rowing across lakes and bays—to say nothing of his climbing, sailing, swimming, trekking, picnicking, bird watching, and gardening—was legendary. He was by all accounts "the greatest sportsman of his day."

Buchan was one of the most accomplished men of the twentieth century. By turns he was a successful barrister, a respected scholar, a popular journalist, a trusted diplomat, a prolific author, an efficient colonial administrator, an innovative publisher, a progressive politician, a relentless reformer, and an active churchman. Best known for his historical romances and thrilling spy novels—he practically invented the genre—he was also the author of more than a hundred nonfiction works, including an authoritative multivolume history of the First World War and biographies of Oliver Cromwell, Caesar Augustus, Lord Montrose, and Walter Scott.

He was born in Scotland on August 26, 1875, the eldest son of a minister in the Presbyterian Free Church. His early years in the strict Calvinistic manse would shape his worldview and stimulate his imagination for the rest of his life. Following a brilliant academic career at Glasgow and Oxford—during which he wrote prolifically—he went to work as a lawyer in London. He maintained his journalistic and literary interests writing for *Blackwood's* magazine and the *Spectator*.

Always interested in politics, he later accepted an invitation to join the staff of Lord Milner, high commissioner of South Africa following the Boer War. His efficient administrative reforms earned him a trusted place in His Majesty's court and his foreign dispatches earned him renown as one of the British Empire's finest correspondents.

Following his tenure in the foreign service, he was offered lucrative posts as a director of the Edinburgh publishing firm Thomas Nelson and of the international news service Reuters. He published several highly acclaimed novels and historical studies. When war broke out in Europe, however, he set aside his wide-ranging pursuits to join the British Intelligence Corps as a department director.

After the First World War he was elected to Parliament representing the Scottish universities, a position he held until 1935. Meanwhile he resumed his flourishing literary career—between 1922 and 1936 he averaged five books a year. For much of that time he was ranked among the world's best-selling authors alongside his close friends Rudyard Kipling, Virginia Wolfe, G. K. Chesterton, Hilaire Belloc, and Hugh Walpole. Several of his books, including *The Thirty-Nine Steps*, *Prester John*, *Huntingtower*, and *John McNab*, were even made into full-length motion pictures by the likes of Alfred Hitchcock and Arthur Lammis. Though his work was popular, it often explored serious theological themes and profound human dilemmas. Indeed, according to T. E. Lawrence, he was "the greatest romancer of our blind and undeserving generation."

Throughout the crowded hours of his career he maintained a vital interest in both his family and his faith. He was married in 1907 to Susan Grosvenor and together they had a daughter and three sons. Though always maintaining a busy schedule, he made certain that his children remained priority in their parents' lives. Likewise, he was a faithful member of the Presbyterian Church, serving his congregation as a Bible study leader and elder for most of his adult life.

His political, cultural, and spiritual prominence made him an appropriate choice as the king's lord high commissioner to the General Assembly of the Church of Scotland for several years beginning in 1933. The post enabled him to promote the vital relationship between the dynamics of the Christian life and the preservation of Western civilization—a relationship he believed was threatened by the hubris of modern secularism. It was a theme that resonated throughout all his work. "Our enemies are attacking more than our system of Christian morals on which our civilization is founded," he lamented. "They are attacking Christianity itself, and they are succeeding. Our great achievements in perfecting the scientific apparatus of life have tended to produce a mood of self-confidence and pride. We have too often become gross materialists in our outlook on life."

Despite this obvious twentieth-century cultural retrogression, Buchan remained confident. "I believe that the challenge with which we are faced may restore us to that manly humility in the presence of the Unseen which alone gives power," he said. "It may bring us back to God. In that case our victory is assured. The church of Christ is an anvil which has worn out many hammers. Our opponents may boast of their strength, but they do not realize what they have challenged."

His tireless activities on behalf of Christ and Crown brought him greater and greater prominence and despite deteriorating health he served as Curator of Oxford University Chest, trustee of the National Library of Scotland, president of the Scottish Historical Society, and chancellor of Edinburgh University.

In 1935 King George V ennobled him as the first Lord Tweedsmuir of Elsfield and—at the behest of Prime Minister Mackenzie King—appointed him the fifteenth governor-general of Canada. Despite recurring ill health Buchan threw himself into these new proconsular duties with especial fervor. Moving to Ottawa, he quickly fell in love with the great beauty and diversity of Canada—a land he called "God's manifestation of grace among the nations."

Always an avid outdoorsman, he toured every province and explored every aspect of Canadian life and culture. All of his most beautiful and eloquent writing vibrated to this note of a passionate love of nature. His letters are filled with observations from nature. His speeches made generous use of outdoor allusions and illustrations. His mind was utterly possessed by the glory of the created order. In the tumultuous days during the advent of the Second World War, he became a beloved symbol of faith, stability, and constancy in the face of great evil—a manly stalwart of the land.

His sudden death on February 12, 1940, was caused by a freak injury following a fall in his official Ottawa residence, Rideau Hall. The sad news made front page headlines around the world from South Africa and Australia to Britain and the United States—but nowhere was he mourned as sincerely as in his adopted home. As the historian G. M. Trevelyan commented in the *Globe and Mail*, "I don't think I remember anyone who has died during my lifetime whose death ever had a more enviable outburst of sorrow and love and admiration, public and private. He was the Christian statesman extraordinaire." But even more, "He was," according to his friend Hilaire Belloc, "the quintessential man—a heady dose of masculinity in a world gone soft and frilly. He was the sort of man who instills in us the hope that one day manliness might actually return to lead us out of our cultural dire straits."

What is this beast we call man?
Keeper of the torch of civilization?
Steward of a commonweal of land?
Proclaimer of hope's exaltation?

Protector of hearth and home?
Standard bearer of truth and life?
Revealer of that may be known?
Mediator and progenitor of all strife?

Indeed, such is man, the manly man;
All these and yet still more;
The pedestal upon which we stand;
Lest the West pass into misty lore.

                       John Buchan (1875–1940)

Vision

Vision is the ability to look beyond the constraints of present circumstances to the possibilities of the future. It is the hunger to see what is in terms of what ought to be. It is the passion to live life beyond the limits imposed by the tyranny of the urgent. We live in a pragmatic time of expediency, practicality, and sensibility—as a result, the cause of the visionary is all too often seen as little more than a lost cause. Throughout the ages, however, wise men and women have seen vision for what it is: the hope of the future, the mainspring of progress, and the provocation for success.

It is not the critic that counts; not the man who points out how the strong man stumbles, or where the doer of deeds could have done better. The credit belongs to the man who is actually in the arena, whose face is marred by dust and sweat and blood; who strives valiantly, who errs, and comes short again and again, because there is no effort without error and short-coming; but who does actually strive to do the deeds.

Theodore Roosevelt (1858–1919)

All the evils in our now extensive catalogue flow from a falsified picture of the world which, for our immediate concern, results in an inability to inter-pret current happenings.

Richard Weaver (1910–1963)

We should remember that it is no honor or profit merely to appear in the arena, but the wreath is for those who contend aright.

James A. Garfield (1831–1881)

The streets of hell are paved with good intentions.

Mark Twain (1835–1910)

Some men please themselves with a constant regularity of life, and decency of behavior. Some are punctual in attendance on public worship, and perhaps in the performance of private devotion. Such men are not hypocrites; the virtues which they practice arise from their principles. Their religion is sincere; what is reprehensible is, that it is partial.

Samuel Johnson (1709–1784)

We should learn to see things in a higher light.

Booker T. Washington (1856–1915)

The age is weary with work and gold;
And high hopes wither, and memories wane,
On hearths and altars the fires are dead;
But that brave faith hath not lived in vain.

Frances Brown (1816–1864)

Example is the school of mankind, and they will learn at no other.

Edmund Burke (1729–1797)

For right is right,
Since God is God,
And right the day must prevail;
To doubt is but disloyalty,
To falter is but travail.

For right is right,
Let it be known
And right the day must win;
To dither is but apostasy,
To hesitate is thus sin.

Martin Hever (1766–1839)

Things just don't turn up in this world until someone turns them up.

James A. Garfield (1831–1881)

Those who have not discovered that worldview is the most important thing about a man, as about the men composing a culture, should consider the train of circumstances which have with perfect logic proceeded from this. The denial of universals carries with it the denial of everything transcending experience.

Richard Weaver (1910–1963)

It is natural to mean well, when only abstracted ideas of virtue are proposed to the mind, and no particular passion turns us aside from rectitude; and so willing is every man to flatter himself, that the difference between approving laws, and obeying them is frequently forgotten.

Samuel Johnson (1709–1784)

Learn all you can, but learn to do something, or your learning will be useless and your vision will depart.

Booker T. Washington (1856–1915)

Innocence prolonged ignores experience; knowledge denied becomes a stone in the head.

Andrew Nelson Lytle (1902–1995)

The oppression of the people is a terrible sin; but the depression of the people is far worse.

G. K. Chesterton (1874–1936)

Speak softly and carry a big stick; you will go far. It sounds rather as if that were but a homely old adage, yet as is often the case with matters of tradition, this truism is actually true.

Theodore Roosevelt (1858–1919)

Indifference in questions of importance is no amiable quality.

Samuel Johnson (1709–1784)

A pound of pluck is worth a ton of luck.

James A. Garfield (1831–1881)

The true discoverer is not he who stumbles across that which none else has stumbled but he who beholds its wonder and tells of its glory and makes use of its stewardship.

Seneca (c. 5–65)

What great men do, the less will prattle of.
William Shakespeare (c. 1564–1616)

Those who are quick to promise are generally slow to perform. They promise mountains and perform molehills. He who gives you fair words and nothing more feeds you with an empty spoon. People don't think much of a man's piety when his promises are like pie-crust: made to be broken.
Charles H. Spurgeon (1834–1892)

The most dangerous form of sentimental debauch is to give expression to good wishes on behalf of virtue while you do nothing about it. Justice is not merely words. It is to be translated into living acts.
Theodore Roosevelt (1858–1919)

We are perpetually being told that what is wanted is a strong man who will do things. What is really wanted is a strong man who will undo things; and that will be the real test of strength.
G. K. Chesterton (1874–1936)

Hooey pleases boobs a great deal more than sense.
H. L. Mencken (1880–1956)

The invulnerable thing is not that which is not struck, but that which is not hurt—that which endures if only in aspiration.
Seneca (c. 5–65)

The future is purchased at the price of vision in the present.
Samuel Johnson (1709–1784)

There is only one form of political strategy in which I have any confidence, and that is to try to do the right thing—and sometimes be able to succeed.
Calvin Coolidge (1872–1933)

Behold all the leaders who have been handed down to posterity as instances of an evil fate—yet among them the good, the true, and the great.
Seneca (c. 5–65)

One horse-laugh is worth ten-thousand syllogisms.
H. L. Mencken (1880–1956)

Every great nation owes to the men whose lives have formed part of its greatness not merely the material effect of what they did, not merely the laws they placed upon the statute books or the victories they won over armed foes, but also the immense but indefinable moral influence produced by their deeds and words themselves upon the national character.
Theodore Roosevelt (1858–1919)

For our titanic purposes of faith and revolution, what we need is not the old acceptance of the world as a compromise, but some way in which we can heartily hate and heartily love it. We do not want joy and anger to neutralize each other and produce a surly contentment; we want a fiercer delight and fiercer discontent. We have to feel the universe at once as an ogre's castle, to be stormed, and yet as our own cottage, to which we can return at evening.
G. K. Chesterton (1874–1936)

Sodom was crushed in divine judgment. And why, asks me? Was it due to abomination heaped upon abomination such as those perpetuated against the guests of Lot? Nay, saith Scripture. Was it due to wickedness in commerce, graft in governance, and sloth in manufacture? Nay, saith Scripture. In Ezekiel, thus saith Scripture: "Behold this, the sin-guilt of thine sister Sodom: she and her daughters wrought arrogance, fatness, and ill-concern, but neglected the help of the poor and need-stricken. Thus, they were haughty, committing blasphemy before me. Therefore, I removed them in judgment as all see." Be ye warned by Sodom's ensample. She was crushed in divine judgment simply and solely due to her selfish neglect of the deprived and depressed.

William Booth (1829–1912)

We have been slobbered upon by those who have chewed the mad root's poison, a poison that penetrates to the spirit and rots the soul.

Andrew Nelson Lytle (1902–1995)

If your ship doesn't come in, swim out to it.

Andy Tant (1980–1996)

Cotton Mather and the City on a Hill

Separating fact from fiction, exactitude from nostalgia, and actuality from myth in early American history is often more than a little difficult. Though it is perhaps unwise to have anything like an idealized perception of that great epoch, nevertheless it is difficult to dismiss the breadth and depth of the fledgling colonial culture and the substantive character of the people who populated it. Living in a day when genuine heroes are few and far between—at best—those pioneers and the times they vivified provide a startling contrast.

The fact is colonial America produced an extraordinary number of prodigiously gifted men. From William Byrd and George Wythe to Thomas Hutchinson and William Stith, from Robert Beverley and Edward Taylor to Benjamin Franklin and John Bartram the legacy of the seventeenth century's native-born geniuses remains unmatched. Their accomplishments—literary, scientific, economic, political, and cultural—are staggering to consider. According to historian Paul Johnson, "Never before has one place and one time given rise to so many great men."

Most of us are naturally drawn to the dramatic tales of such men as Washington, Hamilton, Adams, Lee, Laurens, Hancock, and the other leaders of the Revolution. But perhaps even more remarkable are the lives of those who preceded the so-called Founding Fathers—the great Pilgrims and Puritans like Cotton Mather.

It is a cruel irony of history that Mather is generally pictured unsympathetically as the archetype of a narrow and severe intolerance, who proved his mettle by prosecuting the Salem witch debacle of 1692. In fact, he never attended the trials—he lived in the distant town of Boston—and actually denounced them once he saw the tenor they had taken. And as for his Puritanism, it was of the most enlightened sort. Mather was a man of vast learning, prodigious talent, and expansive interests. He owned the largest personal library in the New World—consisting of some 4,000 volumes ranging across the whole spectrum of classical learning. He was also the most prolific writer of his day, producing some 450 books on religion, science, history, medicine, philosophy, biography, and poetry. His style ranged from *Magnalia Christi Americana*, dripping with allusions to classical and modern sources, to the practical and straightforward *Essays to Do Good*, which Benjamin Franklin claimed to be the most influential book ever written in this hemisphere.

He was the pastor of the most prominent church in New England—Boston's North Church. He was active in politics and civic affairs, serving as an advisor to governors, princes, and kings. He taught at Harvard and was instrumental in the establishment of Yale. He was the first native-born American to become a member of the scientific elite in the Royal Society. And he was a pioneer in the universal distribution and inoculation of the smallpox vaccine.

His father, Increase Mather, was the president of Harvard, a gifted writer, a noted pastor, and an influential force in the establishment and maintenance of the second Massachusetts Charter. In his day he was thought to be the most powerful man in New England—in fact, he was elected to represent the colonies before the throne of Charles II in London. But according to many historians, his obvious talents and influence actually pale in comparison to his son's.

Likewise, both of Cotton Mather's grandfathers were powerful and respected men. His paternal grandfather, Richard Mather, helped draw up the *Cambridge Platform*, which provided a constitutional base for the

Congregational churches of New England. And with John Eliot and
Thomas Weld, he prepared the *Bay Psalm Book* which was the first text
published in America, achieved world-wide renown, and remains a classic of
ecclesiastical literature to this day. His maternal grandfather was John
Cotton who wrote the important Puritan catechism for children, *Milk for
Babes*, and drew up the *Charter Template* with John Winthrop as a practical
guide for the governance of the new Massachusetts Colony. The city of
Boston was so named in order to honor him—his former parish work in
England was at St. Botolph's Boston.

According to historian George Harper, together these men laid the
foundations for a lasting "spiritual dynasty" in America. Even so, according
to his life-long admirer Benjamin Franklin, "Cotton Mater clearly outshone them all. Though he was spun from a bright constellation, his light
was brighter still." And according to George Washington, "He was
undoubtedly the Spiritual Father of America's Founding Fathers."

Mather was assuredly a man of splendid talents and varied interests
whose impact covered the whole field of human endeavor, but his greatest
contribution may well have been pioneering a theology of Biblical balance—one that ultimately gave shape to early American culture and life.
Again, according to George Harper: "His supreme achievement lay in
drawing on the perspectives of English Puritans like Richard Baxter and
German Pietists like August Hermann Francke to forge a distinctive
American covenantal theology. This new piety would finally come into its
own with the flowering of evangelicalism in the nineteenth and twentieth
centuries. Mather's ministry bridged the gap between what was and what
was to be."

Though some might doubt the influence of the otherworldly German
Pietism in Mather's thought, there is no doubt that he was able to combine

deep devotion and strident action into a single and cohesive vision for life and ministry that gave a unique tenor to the nascent American mindset. He proclaimed a careful balancing of "word and deed, of hand and heart, of the life in the heavenlies and the life of this earth, of personal piety and corporate responsibility."

Toward the end of 1693 he became convinced that in order to facilitate a spiritual reformation in the life of the American church—and those abroad—a survey of the heretofore untold "mighty works of grace" needed to be made public. Though it would not be published until 1702, *Magnalia Christi Americana* is clearly marked by the concerns of the *fin-de-siècle*—or end of the century—in which it was written.

Ever since men first learned to measure the passing of time, the *fin-de-siècle* has been filled with expectation and portent. Every culture across the globe has invariably attached special significance to the fact that another hundred years have passed. Some because they thought the earth was coming to an end. Some because they thought the earth was coming to a beginning. But all because they thought the earth was coming to something—perhaps even, something significantly new and different.

As the twentieth century comes to an end—and with it, the second millenium since Christ—all those primordial fears, foibles, fancies, and fascinations seem to have redoubled their hold on the attentions of the wise and the foolish alike. Witness, for instance, the vast proliferation of apocalyptic literature: rapture fiction, prophetic speculations, and end times hubbub. Thus, we can probably identify all too well with Mather's concerns as he sat to write.

As at the end of the tenth century, men were frightened by the mendicant movements of barbarians pouring over once safe borders with an alarming prolificacy and profligacy. As at the end of the twelfth century, men were unsettled by the specter of unchecked plagues rampaging through the population. As at the end of the fourteenth century, men were uncertain about those things men are usually most certain of: doctrines and dogmas—their careless admixture of faith and faithlessness had wrought remonstrance, schism, confusion, and inquisition. As at the end of the sixteenth century, men were shaken by the terrible swiftness of geopolitical change—by the revolutionary emergence of startling new alliances, the stirring of age-old animosities, and the plotting of fierce contemporary conspiracies.

The more things change, the more they stay the same. Then, as now, the speculations of men ran to the frantic and the frenetic. Ecstatic eschatalogical significance was read into every change of any consequence—be it of the weather or of the government. Apocalyptic reticence was chided as faithlessness, while practical intransigence was enshrined as faithfulness. Fantastic common wisdom replaced ordinary common sense, and plain selfish serenity replaced plain selfless civility.

Mather wrote three hundred years ago, but he wrote in a time very much like our own. What he wrote was a jeremiad—a stern warning. It is a mode of address that we would do well to hear and heed. Though his subject was a survey of the ecclesiastical history of New England—from the founding at Plymouth, the establishment of culture at Boston, and the erection of institutions like Harvard to the desperate struggles of the frontier, the disputations of heretics like Roger Williams and Anne Hutchinson, and the wars against the Indians—his purpose was the restoration of the original vision of the pioneers who had come to America to "set a city on a hill." Afraid that such a vision had become a kind of lost cause, he desired, first and foremost, to revive the traditions of the "New England way" and the fervor of the old "errand into the wilderness." His fear was that the growing prosperity of the land had "softened the resolve and hardened the hearts" of the "heirs of the Pilgrims and Puritans."

So instead of writing original history, after the fashion of eyewitnesses like Thucydides and Villehardouin, or reflective history, after the fashion of scholastics like Psellus and Livy, or even directive history, after the fashion of propagandists like Arminius or Bonaventure, Mather preferred philosophical history, after the fashion of functionalists like Eusebius and Vasari. While philosophical history is primarily concerned with the forest, original history is concerned with the trees, reflective history is concerned with the roots, and directive history is concerned with the humus. Thus Mather was concerned first and foremost about the landscape, and only secondarily about the flora and fauna that made up its ecology.

His aim was to preserve the practical lessons and profound legacies of Christendom without the petty prejudices of academic fashions or the parsimonious preferences of Enlightenment innovations. He wanted to avoid the trap of noticing everything that went unnoticed in the past while failing to notice all that the past deemed notable. He shunned the kind of modern epic that today is shaped primarily by the banalities of sterile government schools or the fancies of empty theater scenes rather than the realities of historical facts.

At the same time though, he believed that history was a series of lively adventure stories—and thus should be told without the cumbersome intrusion of arcane academic rhetoric or truckloads of extraneous footnotes. In fact, he believed that history was a romantic moral drama in a world gone impersonally scientific—and thus should be told with passion, unction, and verve. To him, the record of the ages was actually philosophy teaching by example—and because however social conditions may change, the great underlying qualities which make and save men and nations do not alter but are the most important example of all. He understood only too well that the past is ever present, giving shape and focus to all our lives—yet it is not what was, but whatever seems to have been, simply because the past, like the future, is part and parcel of the faith. It is no surprise then that he sought to comprehend events through the same worldview lens as those who wrought the events in the first place.

Religion hath brought forth prosperity, and the daughter destroyed the mother—there is a danger, lest the enchantments of this world make them forget their errand into the wilderness: to build a city on a hill, an illumination for all the world.

❧ *Cotton Mather (1663–1728)* ☙

Domesticity

*T*here is no place like home. Of joy, of peace, of plenty, where supporting and supported, dear souls mingle into the blissful hubbub of daily life. No matter how benevolent, no matter how philanthropic, and no matter how altruistic some social or cultural alternative may be, it can never hope to match the personal intimacy of domestic relations. Except in the rare and extreme cases where strife and bitterness have completely disintegrated familial identity, there is no replacement for the close ties of brothers and sisters, fathers and mothers, husbands and wives, parents and children, aunts and uncles, kith and kin. Though under siege in our day, domesticity has always been recognized as the glue that holds nations together—and ever it shall be.

The strength and glory of a land does not depend upon its wealth, its defenses, its great houses, its powerful armaments; but on the number of its gracious, serious, kind, and wise citizens.

Martin Luther (1483–1546)

It is impossible for any culture to be sound and healthy without a proper respect and proper regard for the soil.

Andrew Nelson Lytle (1902–1995)

One of the strangest disparities of history lies between the sense of abundance felt by older and simpler societies and the sense of scarcity felt by the ostensibly richer societies of today. Perhaps the difference is the loss of community that so afflicts us today—in stark contrast to those happier cultures of days gone by.

Richard Weaver (1910–1963)

Hearth and home are the cornerstones of help and hope and happiness.

Mark Twain (1835–1910)

The lowest subdivision of society, is that by which it is broken into private families; nor do any duties demand more to be explained and enforced, than those which this relation produces; because none are more universally obligatory, and perhaps very few are more frequently neglected.

Samuel Johnson (1709–1784)

Any woodsman can tell you that in a broken and sundered nest, one can hardly expect to find more than a precious few whole eggs. So it is with the family.

Thomas Jefferson (1743–1826)

No other success in life—not being President, or being wealthy, or going to college, or anything else—comes up to the success of the man and woman who can feel that they have done their duty and that their children and grandchildren rise up to call them blessed.

Theodore Roosevelt (1858–1919)

Do not bemoan the turn of fortune that makes of a simple matter a heroic act.

Andrew Nelson Lytle (1902–1995)

Politics is important. But it is not all-important. That is not just a modern phenomenon. It has always been a fact of life. Many who live and die by the electoral sword will certainly be shocked to discover that most of the grand-glorious headline-making events in the political realm today will go down in the annals of time as mere backdrops to the real drama of everyday banalities. But it is so. As much emphasis as is placed on campaigns, primaries, caucuses, conventions, elections, statutes, administrations, surveys, polls, trends, and policies these days, most of us know full well that the import of fellow workers, next door neighbors, close friends, and family members is actually far greater. Despite all the hype, hoopla, and hysteria of sensational turns-of-events, the affairs of ordinary people who tend their gardens and raise their children and perfect their trades and mind their businesses are, in the end, more important. Just like they always have been. Just like they always will be.

Tristan Gylberd (1954–)

I know a beautiful lovely garden. There are many children in it picking up apples under the trees, and pears, cherries, and plums; they sing, hop about and are happy. I asked a man whose garden it was whose children they were. He answered: they are the children that like to pray and learn and are pious—as would be the case in any garden in this world, of course.

Martin Luther (1483–1546)

There is need to develop all the virtues that have the state for their sphere of action; but these virtues are as dust in a windy street unless back of them lie the strong and tender virtues of a family life based upon the love of the one man for the one woman and on their joyous and fearless acceptance of their common obligation to the children that are theirs.

Theodore Roosevelt (1858–1919)

According to the Word of God, the family is portrayed as the wonderful creation through which the rich fabric of our organic human life must spin itself out.

Abraham Kuyper (1837–1920)

The family is the true society.

of Pope Leo XIII (1810–1903) fo

The tasks of family in society lie outside government's jurisdiction. With those it is not to meddle.

of Abraham Kuyper (1837–1920) fo

The family is the primary building block of our culture. Nay, it is itself our culture.

of Henry Cabot Lodge (1850–1924) fo

The family is the only means by which real and substantial change for good might truly be effected.

of James Stuart (1849–1901) fo

There is no other place where the human spirit can be so nurtured as to prosper spiritually, intellectually, and temporally, than in the bosom of the family's rightful relation.

of John Chrysostom (c. 344–407) fo

The family is the basic building block of society. When the family begins to break down, the rest of society begins to disintegrate. There is no replacement for the family. The government can't substitute services for it. Social workers can't substitute kindness and understanding for it. Educators can't substitute knowledge, skills, or understanding for (c)it. We need the family. We need fathers, and mothers, and brothers, and sisters. We need grandparents, and aunts, and uncles, and cousins.

Tristan Gylberd (1954–)

Caesars and Satraps attempt to succor our wounds and wants with opulent circuses and eloquent promises. All such dolations are mere pretense, however, in comparison to the genuine Christian care afforded at even the coarsest family hearth.

Methodius (c. 815–885)

Family accountability and discipline bring out the very best in us. A typical mother or father, without thinking twice about it, would willingly die, in a fire or accident, say, in order to save one of his or her children. While in most circumstances this human act would be regarded as heroic, for parents it is only ordinary. Thus the Creator has shaped family life to teach as a matter of course the role of virtue.

Michael Jones (1899–1976)

Family life provides men with a proper sense of identity. In the midst of our families we can know and be known. We can taste the joys and sorrows of genuine intimacy. We can gain a vision of life that is sober and sure. We are bolstered by the love of family. We are strengthened by the confidence of family. We are emboldened by the legacy of family. And we are stabilized by the objectivity of family. In addition, family life provides men with a genuine social security. There's no place like home. In times of trouble our greatest resource will always be those who know us best and love us most. Because family members share a common sense of destiny with one another and a bond of intimacy to one another they can—and will—rush to one another's sides when needed. And well they should.

Tristan Gylberd (1954–)

At a time when liberty is under attack, decency is under assault, the family is under siege, and life itself is threatened, the good will arise in truth; they will arise in truth with the very essence and substance of their lives; they will arise in truth though they face opposition by fierce subverters; they will arise in truth never shying from the Standard of truth, never shirking from the Author of truth.

Henry Laurens (1724–1792)

Happy homes are the responsibility of husbands and fathers—but inevitably it is wives and mothers who make it so.

Theodore Roosevelt (1858–1919)

To be happy at home is the end of all labor.

Samuel Johnson (1709–1784)

The contention that the civil government should at its option intrude into and exercise control over the family and the household is a great and pernicious error.

Pope Leo XIII (1810–1903)

Of all the tyrannies, a tyranny sincerely expressed for the good of its victims may be the most oppressive. It may be better to live under robber barons than under omnipotent ideological busybodies.

C. S. Lewis (1898–1963)

Ownership of the means of production cannot be entrusted to socialistic bureaucrats any more than to monopolistic plutocrats. Three acres and a cow may seem hopelessly out of date as an answer to the cries of the needy—especially in light of the burden of taxation and regulation heaped upon the freeholds of our day. But the great lesson of history is clear enough: when men are left free to faithfully work at home, they are happiest and society is securest.

James Stuart (1849–1901)

True social security affords the broadest distribution of property through legitimate work as is humanly possible.

Abraham Kuyper (1837–1920)

Multiple jurisdictions and free associations are hedges against both tyranny and anarchy, against both cultural hegemony and civil disintegration. The medieval guilds were not collectivist but through communal means they enforced the necessity of upholding interpersonal responsibility and accountability—a profound Christian necessity in light of the deleterious effects of sin on men and man.

Henry Cabot Lodge (1850–1924)

There is a spiritual cancer at work in the world. The piracy of man's fallen nature invariably mitigates against freedom and justice. Therefore voluntary associations must needs balance us—without force of state but nonetheless with force of community—and hold us to accounts.

James Stuart (1849–1901)

A person must be able to earn his living before he can be of much benefit to himself and the community in which he lives.

Booker T. Washington (1856–1915)

Any successful program of social reform requires what called the cooperation of many and diverse elements within the community.
Pope Leo XIII (1810–1903)

Keep steadily in the view of the great principles for which you contend: the
safety of your homes and the lives of all you hold dear depend upon your
courage and exertions. Let each man resolve to be victorious, and that the
right of self-government, liberty, and peace shall find him a defender.
Robert E. Lee (1807–1870)

The most extraordinary thing in the world is an ordinary man and an ordinary woman and their ordinary children.
G. K. Chesterton (1874–1936)

The nameless pioneers and settlers, the obscure mothers and fathers, the
quiet craftsmen and tradesmen; it is only among these that the real story of
America is told; it is only among them that the brilliance of liberty may be
comprehended.
Theodore Roosevelt (1858–1919)

We were born on the same soil, breathe the same air, live on the same land, so why should we not be brothers and sisters?

Nathan Bedford Forrest (1821–1877)

The community is the true sphere of human virtue. In social, active life, difficulties will perpetually be met with; restraints of many kinds will be necessary; and studying to behave right in respect of these, is a discipline of the human heart, useful to others, and improving to itself.

Samuel Johnson (1709–1784)

When, in disgrace with fortune and men's eyes,
I all alone beweep my outcast state,
And trouble deaf heaven with my bootless cries,
And look upon myself and curse my fate,
Wishing me like to one more rich in hope,
Featured like him, like him with friends possessed,
Desiring this man's art and that man's scope,
With what I most enjoy contented least;
Yet in these thoughts myself almost despising,
Haply I think on thee, and then my state,
Like to the lark at break of day arising
From sullen earth, sings hymns at heaven's gate;
    For thy sweet love rememb'red such wealth brings,
    That then I scorn to change my state with kings.

William Shakespeare (c. 1564–1616)

The longing for home is woven into the fabric of our lives and is profoundly effected by our inescapable connection to places, persons, and principles:
the incremental parts of community.

Jonathan Jelliston (1891–1977)

The nomad spirit of modernity has dashed the integrity of community—
but not the deep need for it.

Harold Beekser (1922–1997)

Attachment to the soil is an inescapable aspect of the healthy psyche.
Uprootedness is a kind of psychosis—sadly, rampant in our community-less
society.

Martin Lembec (1909–1990)

The sin of egotism always takes the form of withdrawal. When personal
advantage becomes paramount, the individual passes out of the community.

Richard Weaver (1910–1963)

THOMAS CHALMERS AND THE RECOVERY OF THE PARISH

The great Scottish pastor, social reformer, educator, author, and scientist Thomas Chalmers was born on March 17, 1780, at Anstruther on the Fife coast. His father was a prosperous businessman in the town and Thomas grew up as the sixth in a large family of fourteen children—he had eight brothers and five sisters.

Showing early signs of prodigy, at the age of three he went to the local parish school to learn the classical trivium of grammar, logic, and rhetoric in English, Latin, Greek, and Hebrew. His parents were people of strong Calvinist conviction and keen that their family should grow up to bear witness to a lively and relevant Christianity. Piety and intellectual rigor marked their daily lives.

Before he was twelve he had sufficiently mastered language, literary, and philosophical skills that he was recommended to advance his studies at the University of Saint Andrews. His brother William, who was just thirteen, accompanied him. At the time, Thomas was the second-youngest student at Saint Andrews and widely recognized as a student with extraordinary promise. Although a great part of his time in the first two sessions at the university were apparently occupied in boyish amusements, such as golf, soccer, and handball—in which he was remarkably expert, owing to his being left-handed—he had already begun to demonstrate the great intellectual power which was to be one of his chief characteristics throughout adult life. For mathematics he developed special enthusiasm and to its study he gave himself with great energy and dedication. Ethics and politics were also themes of special interest to him as he sought to integrate his life and faith with the evident woes of the world around him.

In 1795, now fifteen years-old, he sensed a call into the ministry—though as yet still quite immature in his faith—and so he was enrolled as a student of Divinity. That session he actually studied very little theology because having recently taught himself sufficient French to use the language for study, he pursued his researches into theoretical mathematics with renewed vigor. Nevertheless, towards the end of the session he was deeply stirred by the power of the writings of Jonathan Edwards and came to an intellectual grasp of the magnificence of the Godhead and of the providential subordination of all things to His one sovereign purpose.

During these years another part of his great talent began to come into prominence. On entry to the university his expressive proficiency in English grammar and rhetoric was at best immature, but after two years of study, there was a perceptible change. The gifts of powerful, intense, and sustained expression revealed themselves with freedom, spontaneity, and beauty. Student debating societies, class discourses, and daily prayers in the university were all enriched by his tasteful, capable, and eloquent participation.

By 1798, having just reached the age of eighteen, he had completed his course of studies at the University of Saint Andrews. The foundations were laid for his future development. As his biographer Hanna would later assert, "The intensity of his nature, the redundant energy that hardly knew fatigue, the largeness of his view, the warmth of his affection, the independence of his judgement, and the gushing impetuosity of his style, were already manifest from these college days."

In July 1799, he was licensed to preach after a special dispensation exempted him from the qualifying condition of having reached the age of twenty-one. At the same time, he became a teaching assistant at the University of Edinburgh in the widely varied disciplines of mathematics, chemistry, natural and moral philosophy and political economy.

During the winter of 1801, he was offered a post as assistant in the Mathematics Department at Saint Andrews as well as the pastorate of the small parish church in Kilmany. And thus began his remarkable dual career as an ecclesiastic and an academic. Over the next forty-four years Thomas Chalmers gave himself to public service. Twenty of these years were spent in three parishes: first at Kilmany and then later at the Tron Church and Saint John's Church, both in Glasgow. The remaining twenty-four years were spent as a professor in three different chairs, moral philosophy in Saint Andrews, professor of Divinity in Edinburgh, and principal and professor of Divinity in the Free Church Theological Institution, Edinburgh, later known as New College. Often, he served both church and university simultaneously, evoking the wonder of the entire world.

As a teacher, he aroused the enthusiasm of his students. One of them later commented, "Under his extraordinary management, the study of Mathematics was felt to be hardly less a play of the fancy than a labor of the intellect—the lessons of the day being continually interspersed with applications and illustrations of the most lively nature, so that he secured in a singular manner the confidence and attachment of his pupils." Likewise, his parishioners found his sermons to be both erudite and winsome, aimed at both orthodoxy and orthopraxy. His reputation was soon spread throughout Scotland.

The years of work given to parish ministry were extremely significant in the life of Thomas Chalmers. The mental capacity that he had shown in academic pursuits and his youthful strength of spirit were now brought to the test of service to rural and urban communities at a time of extremely significant social change, and the ever transforming power of the Gospel was to prove itself in and through his life and service.

Family bereavements brought Chalmers to reflect more seriously about a dimension of life which, on his own confession, he had not fully considered. His brother George, three years older, and his sister Barbara, some five years older, both died within the space of two years. George had been the captain of a merchant ship but succumbed to tuberculosis and returned home at the age of twenty-nine to die. He awaited the end calmly, his trust resting firmly in Christ. Each evening he had read to him one of John Newton's sermons and obviously derived especial comfort therein. His quiet and assured faith challenged his younger brother. Barbara, suffering the same disease, likewise showed great fortitude and confidence in the face of death. The nature of these circumstances brought him to question his previous conceptions.

After Barbara's death, Thomas, who had been commissioned to write several articles for the Encyclopaedia Britannica on mathematical subjects, wrote to the editor and asked that the article on Christianity should also be allocated to him. Before finishing the article and just after he had made his maiden speech in the General Assembly of 1809, he himself fell gravely ill. Ill-health dogged him for months—at one point being so severe that his family despaired of his very life. The combination of his illness and the loss of his siblings signaled a profound change in his life. He wrote to a friend:

> "My confinement has fixed on my heart a very strong impression of the insignificance of time—an impression which I trust will not abandon me though I again reach the heyday of health and vigor. This should be the first step to another impression still more salutary—the magnitude of eternity. Strip human life of its connection with a higher scene of existence and it is the illusion of an instant, an unmeaning farce, a series of visions and projects, and convulsive efforts, which terminate in nothing. I have been reading Pascal's Thoughts on Religion: you know his history—a man of the richest endowments, and whose

youth was signalized by his profound and original speculations in mathematical science, but who could stop short in the brilliant career of discovery, who could resign all the splendors of literary reputation, who could renounce without a sigh all the distinctions which are conferred upon genius, and resolve to devote every talent and every hour to the defense and illustration of the Gospel. This, my dear sir, is superior to all Greek and Roman fame."

Yet another influence on his spiritual development at this time was the reading of William Wilberforce's *Practical View of Christianity*. Again, he wrote, "The deep views he gives of the depravity of our nature, of our need of an atonement, of the great doctrine of acceptance through that atonement, of the sanctifying influence of the Spirit—these all have given a new aspect to my faith."

Chalmers now had his priorities set in order before him. He gladly recognized God's claim to rule the affections of his heart and command his life's obedience. The remainder of his ministry in Kilmany was profoundly affected by the experience of a vital Christian walk. His preaching had new life and concern, proclaiming what he had formerly disclaimed. His pastoral visitation and his instruction in the homes of his parish showed greater ardor than ever before. From outside the region many came to hear the Word, and heard it gladly. There were innumerable converts to this living Christianity.

Chalmers became an earnest student of the Scriptures and also set aside one day each month when, before God, he reviewed his service to Him and sought, with confession and thanksgiving, the blessing of God on his work and on the people entrusted to his pastoral care. These years were also those of the Napoleonic wars and Chalmers joined the volunteers, holding commissions as a chaplain and lieutenant, though he was never deployed on the continent.

He completely abandoned himself to the covenantal community there at Kilmany. He married and had his first children there. He established a classical school at the heart of the parish. He set about a reform of the ministry to the poor, the widows, and the orphans. He established a pioneer missionary society and a Bible society. In addition, Chalmers began his prodigious and prolific publishing career.

It was inevitable that a man of such gifts would not long be underutilized in the small environs of the Fife seacoast. In July 1815, when news of the victory at Waterloo was scarcely a month old, he preached the last sermon of his twelve-year ministry in Kilmany. His final exhortation was: "Choose Him, then, my brethren. Choose Him as the Captain of your salvation. Let Him enter into your hearts by faith, and let Him dwell continually there. Cultivate a daily intercourse and a growing acquaintance with Him. O you are in safe company, indeed, when your fellowship is with Him."

Thomas Chalmers went to Glasgow at the invitation of the magistrates and town council of Glasgow. He served first in the Tron Church until 1819, and then, by the election of the town council, he was transferred to the newly-created parish of Saint John's, a poorer parish with a very high proportion of factory a workers, a parish in which he had the freedom to develop the ideas that he had long been maturing.

In the later years at Kilmany, Chalmers had made conscience of his work as a parish minister and had come to know the problems of working a rural parish. Now with his newly expanded duties in Glasgow, he came to grips with the difficulties of work in a city parish and applied his intelligence and strength to new problems.

From the beginning of his ministry in the city his preaching was fully appreciated, and many attended from throughout Glasgow, but Chalmers was concerned that his ministry should first and foremost be to the parish—where some eleven or twelve thousand people lived and worked. He commenced a program of visitation from house to house which took two years to complete. He organized the eldership to cooperate in this task and developed Sabbath evening schools. Commencing with thirteen children, the schools grew until within two years they had twelve hundred children under instruction. His awareness of the situation of the people gave him an acute understanding of the problems of illiteracy and poverty in the parish and he could not rest until he had found some means of remedying these. His interest in the working man furthered his reflections on the economic situation; his interest in the sciences led to the Astronomical Discourses, a series of Thursday afternoon sermons delivered once every two months during 1816. Many businessmen and others left their place of work to hear these and during 1817 nine editions of some twenty thousand copies were published.

In 1816 the University of Glasgow unanimously conferred on him the degree of Doctor of Divinity. The lord high commissioner at the General Assembly in the same year invited him to preach in Edinburgh at the time of the assembly. Hard work and new-found fame were joined in the experience of Chalmers, but he was dissatisfied.

He was convinced that the Christian church had as yet unfulfilled responsibilities to all those who lived and worked in the local parish, not merely to those who attended the local place of worship. In the development of Sabbath school work Chalmers discovered that many children had great difficulty in reading. He resolved to remedy the defect by setting up classical schools throughout the parish—especially for the poor and neglected. Provision for the needs of the poor was also made, not from the poor-rate levy, but from funds administered by the church of the parish through its deacons who were given special training for this work. Relatives of the needy were encouraged to assume responsibility and the government's poor relief costs for the parish were reduced by more than eighty percent within three years. And as if all this were not enough, by correspondence he maintained a ministry with many others beyond the bounds of Glasgow, writing on average some fifty letters a week—and they were, for the most part, letters of great substance.

The years of his ministry in Glasgow were very significant. There was no class of persons untouched by his labors. Before his time many had fallen away from all Christian belief and observance, but under his ministry public sentiment turned decisively to evangelical liveliness. By his labors living faith in Christ was restored and many men and women throughout the city gave themselves for Christian service.

When he was invited to return to his former University, Saint Andrews, as professor of moral philosophy, he accepted because he saw it as a position of wider usefulness and also because he felt that the pressure of life in Glasgow which had progressively increased was making excessive demands on him. But his concerns for the urban parishes remained undiminished. His interest, for instance, in dealing with the problem of poverty led to an invitation to London by the Parliamentary Committee on the Irish Poor Law. In 1840 he gave a paper at the British Association for the Advancement of Science recommending the system of voluntary assistance to the poor. He was well informed on the major public issues of his day— Roman Catholic Emancipation, the Reform Bill, and the Corn Laws—and his opinion was valued by great and small alike on all of these problems. In 1832 the bishop of London recommended the president of the Royal

Society to invite Dr. Chalmers to prepare a treatise in proof of the wisdom and benevolence of God shown in the works of creation. It was published in the following year with funds from the legacy of the earl of Bridgewater and was known as the Bridgewater Treatise.

Amongst the honors that had come his way in the same year was his election as moderator of the General Assembly of the Church of Scotland. He had previously formed part of a delegation on William IV's accession in 1830 and had been named as one of His Majesty's chaplains in Scotland. He was later to present a loyal address on behalf of the University of Edinburgh to Queen Victoria on her accession in 1837. In January 1834 Dr. Chalmers was elected a Fellow of the Royal Society of Edinburgh and the following year became one of its vice-presidents. The Royal Institute of France honored him with the title of Corresponding Member and four years later, in 1838, he visited France and read a lecture on the "Distinction both in principle and effect between a legal charity for the relief of indigence and a legal charity for the relief of disease." His many books and sermons were invariably bestsellers for years on end.

Thus his reputation was well established, his contribution to the life of Scotland, England, and Ireland fully recognized, and his fame spread around the world when he found himself not only involved in, but leading, a movement that was to divide the Church of Scotland, and to set him in apparent disregard of the authority of the highest civil court in the land.

With the disappearance of the Roman Catholic Church in Scotland as a spiritual force in the sixteenth century, the Presbyterian Church had assumed the right to be the Church of Scotland. Its struggle for spiritual independence had been a long and costly one under the leadership of John Knox, Andrew Melville, and Alexander Henderson amongst others. At long last, in 1690, the Presbyterian Church was legally recognized by the crown as the established Church of Scotland, but in this recognition by the state there was no question of the church surrendering any aspect of its independence. It was free to follow the guidance of the Divine Head in every aspect in which He had expressed His will.

Patronage, or the right of landowners to bring to a parish a minister who might or might not be acceptable to the elders and members of it, had been brought in by act of Parliament in 1712. But in 1838, in two cases in particular, those of Auchterarder and Marnoch, ministers were forced on congregations opposed to their settlement and the Court of Session and the House of Lords ratified these decisions. Many in the church were seriously perturbed.

There were other areas of concern as well. It was decided that the Church did not have the power to organize new parishes nor give the ministers there the status of clergy of the Church. It had no authority to receive again clergy who had left it. And perhaps worst of all a creeping liberal formalism was slowly smothering the evangelical zeal of the whole land. Alas, despite repeated requests, the government refused to take action to deal with the threat of spiritual atrophy. After a ten-year-long struggle to regain the soul of the church, the evangelical wing led by Chalmers and others laid a protest on the table of the assembly, and some four hundred ministers and a like number of elders left the established Church of Scotland on May 18, 1843, to form the Free Church.

When the General Assembly of the Free Church was constituted that grave morning, Thomas Chalmers was called to be its moderator. He was the man whose reputation in the Christian world was the highest; he was also the man whose influence in directing the events leading to what would eventually be called the Disruption had been greatest.

The ministers who left the Established Church with Chalmers that day sacrificed much. In the personal sphere their houses and financial security were set aside, their work had to be reorganized, and new centers for preaching found. Chalmers, in this respect, also suffered loss. He was no longer professor of Divinity at the University of Edinburgh and the influence and prestige of that position went to another. But the Church realized that, without continued pastoral training, its future was bleak. A center for theological study, the Free Church Theological Institute, was opened and Chalmers was appointed principal and professor of Divinity.

A few years before, when Chalmers had completed his sixtieth year, he looked forward to a "sabbatical decennium," a seventh decade of life that would be spent as "the Sabbath of our earthly pilgrimage—as if on the shore of the eternal world." The years before 1843 had brought him little of the rest and peace that he hoped for and, of course, after the Disruption he had even more to do.

His lectures continued, but there was also the concern of finding a site and constructing a building to house the New College. In 1846, after much personal sacrifice and intense labor, Chalmers laid the foundation stone of the new building. "We leave to others the passions and politics of this world, and nothing will ever be taught, I trust, in any of our halls which shall have the remotest tendency to disturb the existing order of things, or to confound the ranks and distinctions which at present obtain in society. But there is one equality between man and man which will strenuously be taught—the essential equality of human souls; and that in the high count and reckoning of eternity, the soul of the poorest of nature's children, the raggedest boy that runs along the pavement, is of like estimation in the eyes of heaven with that of the greatest and noblest of our land."

The means for supporting the ministers of the church following the Disruption had to be found and Chalmers dedicated much of his time and energy to the setting up of a Sustentation Fund. By the end of 1844 it was clear that the cost of maintaining spiritual independence would involve foregoing any financial assistance given by the state. It was under his leadership that this problem was confronted and resolved. In addition, new sites for some seven hundred churches and manses had to be found for the congregations that were formed, and there were difficulties with several landowners in getting sites. In many cases Chalmers was able to give assistance through his personal influence. His own home in Morningside was used as a place of worship for years afterward.

All this effort was not dedicated simply to perpetuating an idea, for Chalmers had a vision of Scotland in which all her people from those of highest to those of lowest rank would know and love the Lord Jesus Christ. Perhaps the dearest example of the outworking of this vision is seen in the West Port experiment in Edinburgh, "a fourth part of the whole population being pauper and another fourth street beggars, thieves and prostitutes." The population amounted to upwards of 400 families of whom 300 had no connection with the Church. Of 411 children of school age, 290 were growing up without any education. The plan of Chalmers was to divide the whole territory into twenty districts each containing about twenty families. To each district a discipler was appointed whose duty was to visit each family once a week. A school was provided. By the end of 1845, 250 scholars had attended the school. A library, a savings bank, a wash house, and an industrial school had been provided, and there was a congregation served by a missionary-minister. Chalmers often attended the services there and would take part as a worshiper alongside the people of the district.

Thomas Carlyle said of him: "What a wonderful old man Chalmers is. Or rather, he has all the buoyancy of youth. When so many of us are wringing our hands in hopeless despair over the vileness and wretchedness of the large towns, there goes the old man, shovel in hand, down into the dirtiest puddles of the West Port of Edinburgh, cleans them out, and fills the sewers with living waters. It is a beautiful sight."

At the end of the college session in 1847, Chalmers, by now exhausted in his ceaseless labors, went to London on the business of the Church. He returned to his home in Morningside to prepare for the General Assembly on the following Monday. It was after family worship on Sunday evening, May 30, that he said goodnight. He went to sleep in Morningside, but he awoke in Heaven.

The funeral was held on the following Friday, June 4. The magistrates and town council, the members of the assembly, the professors of New College, ministers, probationers, students, the rector and masters of the high school and many thousands more joined the funeral procession, paying their tribute, as they followed the cortege to Grange Cemetery. According to Carlyle: "There was a moral sublimity in the spectacle. It spoke more emphatically than by words of the dignity of intrinsic excellence, and of the height to which a true man may attain. It was the dust of a Presbyterian minister which the coffin contained, and yet they were burying him amid the tears of a nation, and with more than kingly honors."

The smiling little cottage, where at eve
He meets his rosy children at the door,
Prattling their welcomes, and his honest wife,
With good brown cake and bacon slice, intent
To cheer his hunger after labor hard:
Such is the heart, the soul, the very essence,
Of parish life: the hearth, the home, domesticity.

Thomas Chalmers (1780–1847)